BUILDING A K-12 STEM LAB

A STEP-BY-STEP GUIDE FOR SCHOOL LEADERS AND TECH COACHES

DEBORAH KANTOR NAGLER

AND MARTHA OSEI-YAW

INTERNATIONAL SOCIETY FOR TECHNOLOGY IN EDUCATION
PORTLAND, OR · ARLINGTON, VA

DEDICATION

To Fred

—Deborah

To Erika and Jonathan

—Martha

BUILDING A K-12 STEM LAB

A Step-by-Step Guide for School Leaders and Technology Coaches
Deborah Kantor Nagler and Martha Osei-Yaw

ACQUISITIONS AND DEVELOPMENT EDITOR: Valerie Witte
COPY EDITOR: Steffi Drewes
PROOFREADER: Linda Laflamme
INDEXER: Valerie Haynes Perry
BOOK DESIGN AND PRODUCTION: Danielle Foster
COVER DESIGN: Eddie Ouellette

LIBRARY OF CONGRESS CATALOGING-IN-PUBLICATION DATA AVAILABLE

FIRST EDITION
ISBN: 978-1-56484-700-3
Ebook version available
Printed in the United States of America
ISTE® is a registered trademark of the International Society for Technology in Education.

ABOUT ISTE

The International Society for Technology in Education (ISTE) is the premier non-profit organization serving educators and education leaders committed to empowering connected learners in a connected world. ISTE serves more than 100,000 education stakeholders throughout the world.

ISTE's innovative offerings include the ISTE Conference & Expo, one of the biggest, most comprehensive edtech events in the world—as well as the widely adopted ISTE Standards for learning, teaching, and leading in the digital age and a robust suite of professional learning resources, including webinars, online courses, consulting services for schools and districts, books, and peer-reviewed journals and publications. Visit iste.org to learn more.

JOIN OUR COMMUNITY OF PASSIONATE EDUCATORS

ISTE members get free year-round professional development opportunities and discounts on ISTE resources and conference registration. Membership also connects you to a network of educators who can instantly help with advice and best practices.

Join or renew your ISTE membership today!

Visit iste.org/membership or call 800.336.5191.

RELATED ISTE TITLES

Integrating Technology in the Classroom: Tools to Meet the Needs of Every Student
Boni Hamilton

Reinventing Project-Based Learning: Your Field Guide to Real-World Projects in the Digital Age
Suzie Boss and Jane Krauss

To see all books available from ISTE, please visit iste.org/resources.

ABOUT THE AUTHORS

 **DR. DEBORAH KANTOR NAGLER** is an adjunct professor of Educational Technology at New Jersey City University, a lecturer, and a writer. Her recent work in Educational Technology builds upon a career in school and nonprofit administration. Nagler holds an MS in Education Media Design & Technology from Full Sail University and an Ed.D. in Educational Technology Leadership from New Jersey City University, where her research focused on women's participation in makerspaces. She has served as a STEM consultant at several urban public schools in the New York/New Jersey area. Nagler is an instructional designer, a highly experienced trainer, and an explorer of new media and technology, promoting entrepreneurship and invention coupled with positive values. In addition to makerspaces, her interests include game design in virtual reality.

 **DR. MARTHA OSEI-YAW** serves as the principal of Alexander D. Sullivan Elementary School, a bilingual STEM model school. As an adjunct at New Jersey City University, she introduces future educators to innovative ways of integrating technology into the curriculum. She completed both her undergraduate degree and an Ed.D. in Educational Technology Leadership at New Jersey City University. She has also earned an MA from Seton Hall University in Bilingual and Bicultural Education, and another MA in Urban Leadership from Saint Peter's University. She is the co-author of "Challenges in Technology and Its Influence on Education and Training," which was featured in the *Journal of Applied Learning Technology* (2015). In March 2016, she was honored as the "Featured Woman in Technology" by the Hudson County Community College at the Girls in Technology Symposium. Osei-Yaw's professional aspiration is to encourage girls and underrepresented students to pursue careers in Science, Technology, Engineering, and Math (STEM).

ACKNOWLEDGMENTS

To begin, we want to offer a heartfelt thanks to the Jersey City Public School district and the Alexander D. Sullivan School community, whose support helped make the school's STEM Lab possible. We would especially like to thank Dr. Joseph Cordero, Dr. Darrell Carson, and the dedicated teachers and staff at the A.D. Sullivan School for providing access and creating pathways for learning that enable our students to thrive in the study of Science, Technology, Engineering, and Math (STEM). Our thanks, as well, to Michael Burghoff and the staff of PicoTurbine International, who were also contributors to the development of the lab and its programs.

This book began with our experience at the Alexander D. Sullivan School and grew to include the input of several dozen educators. We offer our deepest appreciation to everyone who took time from busy schedules to speak with us about their STEM Lab dreams and achievements. We know that you share our vision for active, authentic STEM learning for every student in every school. We hope that their words and the personal vignettes in each chapter will inspire others to take steps toward project-based learning in a STEM Lab.

To our editor, Valerie Witte, thank you for the encouragement and support. Your patience and guidance have been instrumental in making this volume possible. Thank you to ISTE publications for welcoming and encouraging our work, and to Steffi Drewes, Linda Laflamme, Danielle Foster, and Eddie Ouellette for your contributions.

Finally, we offer a few words of gratitude to the teams behind the scenes—our families.

From Deborah: Thank you to Fred Nagler, my husband, partner, and inspiration in all things, including STEM education. Your patience, perspective, and encouragement have made this book possible.

From Martha: Thank you to my loving family and my intimate circle of friends. Erika, my beautiful daughter, you have always been a source of inspiration. You are one of the reasons that I decided to pursue a career in education over 27 years ago. Jonathan, my amazing husband, you have stood by my side and provided unconditional support throughout this entire journey. Thank you for always believing in me.

CONTRIBUTORS

Alice Nudelman, Immaculate Heart Academy, Washington Twp., NJ

Bret States, San Joaquin DOE, San Joaquin, CA

Chani Lichtiger, Yavneh Academy, Paramus, NJ

Dave Janosz, Northern Valley BOE & Regional High School, Demarest, NJ

David Rackliff, Emek Hebrew Academy, Sherman Oaks, CA

Felicia Cullars, STEM/STEAM Georgia DOE, Atlanta, GA

Gary Menchel, Yeshiva Har Torah, Queens, NY

Kirk Brown, San Joaquin DOE, San Joaquin, CA

Janet Elder, Christa McAuliffe School, Jersey City, NJ

Steve Freedman, Hillel Day School, Farmington Hills, MI

Jonathan Knapp, Yavneh Academy, Paramus, NJ

Marcos Navas, Union City Public Schools, Union City, NJ

Meghan McFerrin, STEM/STEAM Georgia DOE, Atlanta, GA

Norma Fernandez, Jersey City Public Schools, Jersey City, NJ

Orly Nadler, Ma'ayanot Yeshiva High School for Girls, Teaneck, NJ

Patricia Holzman, A. Harry Moore School, Jersey City, NJ

Randall Palmer, Spectrum360, Verona, NJ

Rifkie Silverman, The Frisch School, Paramus, NJ

Rolando Monserrat, Teaneck High School, Teaneck, NJ

Stephanie Talalai, A. Harry Moore School, Jersey City, NJ

Tikvah Wiener, The Idea School, Englewood Cliffs, NJ

CONTENTS

6 AT THE INTERSECTION OF STEM LAB AND CURRICULUM 65

7 READY, SET . . . NOW IMPLEMENT 79

8 IMPACT AND EXPECTATIONS 95

INTRODUCTION

As I approached the room an enthusiastic cheer broke through the air. This was not a rock concert or in a stadium. This sound, bursting through the door of the STEM Lab, was the full voice of third-grade students appreciating a lesson in Biochemistry. Their excitement confirmed for me the power of hands-on learning in STEM.

—MARTHA OSEI-YAW,
PRINCIPAL, A.D. SULLIVAN SCHOOL

YOU ARE HERE

All helpful road maps have a starting point. This book began in the STEM Lab at the A.D. Sullivan School. Often STEM Labs can be found in affluent communities or in schools that focus only on high-performing or advanced learners. A.D. Sullivan is neither of those. It is an urban, bilingual primary school serving a primarily economically disadvantaged population. Eighty-two percent of its students are Hispanic and African-American. More than a quarter of the students have limited English proficiency and 12 percent of the students have special needs. A.D. Sullivan classes meet in a nearly century-old building, the school operates on a below-average budget, and it has **a highly successful STEM program including a STEM Lab**. If they can do it, so can you (Figure I.1).

FIGURE I.1 Students at work in the A.D. Sullivan STEM Lab.

Neither of us began our careers as STEM experts. Martha comes from a public education background and Deborah from a private school and nonprofit administration background. For each of us the STEM turning point was a moment of understanding about how important STEM is to education and the future of our students. This led to enrollment in a doctoral program for Educational Technology Leadership, where we met and began our collaboration. We share our story because there may be those among you who fear that you don't know enough about STEM to build a STEM Lab. The answer is quite simple: Go and learn.

In addition to our academic studies, we took every opportunity to explore STEM education in the field. We attended and presented at conferences, visited numerous STEM Labs, volunteered to help with community-wide programs, and participated in a variety of STEM committees and online communities. One thing we learned is that no one can know everything there is to know about STEM or STEAM; and you do not need to be a STEM expert to begin the work of building a STEM Lab. The best things to do are to continue learning and to gather the best possible expertise around you. Building a successful STEM Lab requires teamwork.

ISTE EDUCATION LEADER STANDARDS

This book is designed to complement the 2018 ISTE Standards for Education Leaders (Appendix A), which serve as a theoretical framework "supporting digital age learning, creating technology-rich learning environments and leading the transformation of the educational landscape" (International Society for Technology in Education [ISTE], 2018). In each chapter, selected standards will be highlighted in a text box alongside the corresponding material. Here is an example:

ISTE STANDARD
VISIONARY PLANNER

Leaders engage others in establishing a vision, strategic plan, and ongoing evaluation cycle for transforming learning with technology. Education leaders:

2e. Share lessons learned, best practices, challenges and the impact of learning with technology with other education leaders who want to learn from this work.

This standard exactly reflects our goal for this book: to share what we, and others, have learned while building and researching STEM Labs. The full text of the Education Leader Standards is available in Appendix A.

WHY STEM?

School labs are not a new phenomenon. Many of you reading this book could describe experiences in the chemistry or biology lab, in shop and in home economics. What differentiates the STEM Lab from previous generations of labs? The answer, in a word, is STEM. STEM is the widely known acronym for Science, Technology, Engineering, and Mathematics. Dr. Judith Ramaley, Assistant Director of the Education and Human Resources Directorate at the National Science Foundation (NSF), first coined the term STEM in the context of discussions of workforce needs in a highly unpredictable and quickly evolving technological environment (Chute, 2009). In 2005, the U.S. National Academies of Science, Engineering, and Medicine (NASEM) issued a report titled "Rising Above the Gathering Storm." Highlighting the connection between economic success and STEM professions, this report stated: "Our primary and secondary schools do not seem able to produce enough students with the interest, motivation, knowledge, and skills they will need to compete and prosper in an emerging world" (Committee on Prospering in the Global Economy, 2007, p. 94). Another existing challenge identified in the report is the need to prepare math and science teachers to better support K–12 students.

The popular conclusion was that a universally strong STEM education would be the best way to achieve the goal of a well-prepared workforce. A Congressional STEM Education Caucus, formed in 2003, then challenged the educational establishment to improve STEM learning. They described the challenge as follows: "Our knowledge-based economy is driven by constant innovation. The foundation of innovation lies in a dynamic, motivated and well-educated workforce equipped with STEM skills" (Our knowledge-based economy, n.a., para. 1).

In the years following the NASEM report, numerous studies analyzed the level and effectiveness of STEM education in schools around the globe. Students in the United States ranked below their counterparts in many other nations (Barshay, 2018; DeSilver, 2017). In response, national and state leaders set out to understand and define effective STEM education, in order to develop pathways for improving STEM education and increasing the number of STEM-trained professionals for the marketplace. One outcome of these efforts was a frequently used definition of STEM education as:

An interdisciplinary approach to learning where rigorous academic concepts are coupled with real-world lessons as students apply science, technology, engineering, and mathematics in contexts that make connections between school, community, work, and the global enterprise enabling the development of STEM literacy and with it the ability to compete in the new economy. (Tsupros, Kohler, & Hallinen, 2009)

The goal of STEM Education was to bring together the study of these four disciplines in a learning construct that takes advantage of the best tools that education in the digital age has to offer.

DEFINING AND UNDERSTANDING STEM EDUCATION

Constructionism, an educational theory developed by Dr. Seymour Papert, provides the foundation for STEM Education as defined above. Constructionism suggests that students learn "by actively constructing knowledge through the act of making something shareable" (Martinez & Stager, 2013, p. 21). Papert asserted that Constructionist theory was confluent with John Dewey's vision of educational environments where "learning is achieved through experimentation, practice, and exposure to the real world" (Papert, 1993, para. 11). Technology, in Papert's view, offers the exact tools necessary to convert Dewey's epistemology into an accessible, practical reality. Most importantly, he saw the role of technology as part of a movement for educational change that will be led by "an army of agents," the students themselves (Papert, 1993, para. 11).

Where the definition of STEM Education speaks about teaching "rigorous academic concepts," Papert spoke about the powerful ideas that are an inherent part of learning science and mathematics (Tsupros, Kohler, & Hallinen, 2009). His concern was that teachers might use technology to continue to teach the same rote applications in the same way they had before technology was available. Papert encouraged teachers to continue to develop their own STEM literacy so that through their teaching an understanding of "powerful advanced ideas" could be facilitated at every level (Papert, 1993).

STEM education applies project-based learning as a means of producing concrete solutions for real-world problems. This is what Jerome Bruner (1966) described as authentic learning involving "deep immersion in consequential activity" (Dougherty, 2016, p. 184). This methodology is the primary delivery system for STEM Education. Among the components of project-based learning are: the composition of driving questions by the students, inquiry-based study, the use of design thinking for developing artifacts of learning, collaboration both between students and with professionals, and use of tools and technology relevant to the field (Bennett, 2014). The teacher lends support by facilitating and keeping records throughout the project. The students take the role of STEM professional preparing, implementing, sharing, and reflecting upon their work.

A growth mindset is the final critical element in successful STEM Education and preparation for a changing and unpredictable work environment. Communication, collaboration, and critical thinking are identifiable as necessary 21st century competencies (P21.org, 2018). At the same time, exploration, experimentation, and innovation, the principal tools of STEM professionals, also require the cultivation of emotional competencies including resilience, persistence, and self-efficacy. Growth mindset, a theory established by Dr. Carol Dweck (2009), recognizes that emotions can influence how we think and that our skills can be improved with effort." Dweck proposes that learners who believe that they can become smarter by making an effort will, in fact, invest the time and effort necessary for success (Mindset Works, 2017).

Failing forward is another important element of STEM education. An example is Deborah's experience with fourth-grade students in the Junior Chapter of the Society of Hispanic Professional Engineers (SHPE) at A.D. Sullivan. They meet twice a month after school in the STEM Lab. On this particular day, the students were engaged in creating load-bearing geodesic domes out of toothpicks and gumdrops. One little boy became weepy when his group's structure collapsed. His teammates quickly consoled him, saying: "It's okay. We can do it again. I know we can do it better this time. Let's try." As Deborah observed this interaction, she thought that it might have been one of the best lessons learned that day, namely that of peers encouraging one another to be resilient and persistent. Grit is an important quality and a key component for a growth mindset (Hochanadel & Finamore, 2015).

To summarize the scope and benefits of STEM Education: It is constructionist, allowing the learner to construct meaning by engaging in hands-on exploration of powerful ideas and technology-supported experimentation; it is project-based, engaging the learner in creating authentic solutions for real-world problems; and it provides a rich environment for cultivating "non-cognitive competencies" that are critical for success in the digital-age workplace. Most STEM-related professions are projected to grow at a much faster rate than other professions over the next 10 years (Bureau of Labor

Statistics, 2018). At the same time, even those who are not engaged in STEM professions will need to apply technology and can derive benefit from a quality STEM Education. There is a growing number of educational leaders, ourselves included, who believe that STEM Education has the potential to promote much-needed change in our schools and that the STEM Lab is the engine that can drive that change. Dave Janosz, the Supervisor of the Technology and Engineering Department for the Northern Valley School District in Demarest, New Jersey, captured this potential in a quote from a student walking into the school's STEM Lab for the first time: "Finally a classroom doesn't look like the 1970s."

WHAT IS A STEM LAB, AND WHY IS IT IMPORTANT?

To be clear, the STEM Lab we are speaking of is a space dedicated to hands-on, project-based, and inquiry-based learning that is integrated with the school's curriculum. Of course, STEM learning can and does take place in classroom spaces. The difference between a classroom and a STEM Lab is that the latter is designed to provide the tools and facilities for STEM experimentation in a space that is shared by the school community. It is both a locus for STEM Education within the school and a place where the product of STEM learning can be shared. The STEM Lab has the potential to be an engine for change encouraging STEM exploration throughout the school, an environment that encourages interdisciplinary, project-based learning in all areas of study, and an exemplar of digital age education at its best. The excitement and energy generated in a STEM Lab can be contagious!

For the purposes of this book, the term STEM Lab is used in its broadest sense. The Lab can have either a STEM or a STEAM focus, depending on the objectives of the particular school. As we discovered in the course of our research, while the A in STEAM most often stands for Art, in some schools it can also signify Architecture or Agriculture. The STEM Lab at the Spectrum360 School includes a green room for photography and film production, while the STEM Lab at the Hillel School in Detroit includes a greenhouse for learning about ecology, micro-agronomy, and health.

The names of these STEM Labs are as varied as their contents. Innovation Lab, Fab Lab, Imagination Station, STEAM Hub, and Project & Idea Realization Lab are just a few of the creative titles that are assigned to these spaces. More important than the moniker, however, is the purpose of your STEM Lab. It must be guided by a clear vision and developed according to specific, standards-supported goals that align with your curriculum. This process will be discussed at length throughout the book.

One frequently asked question is, what is the difference between a STEM Lab and a makerspace? The confusion comes from the fact that there is often overlap in the kinds of equipment, tools, materials, and activities that can be found in both. In fact, some schools refer to their labs as makerspaces and others have a dedicated makerspace area within their STEM Lab. In our view, the key differentiator is purpose. A school-based STEM Lab provides activities that are consciously aligned and integrated with the school curriculum. Activity in a STEM Lab is structured inquiry that is vetted or facilitated by teachers, and is aligned with standards. A makerspace, on the other hand, offers the opportunity for unfettered play, exploration, tinkering, and creative self-expression. Dougherty (2016) describes the difference: "Project-based learning can be aligned with making, but there is an important difference. If students are doing hands-on activity at the direction of the teacher, often to support a curriculum goal, it is not a maker project" (p. 179).

As Laura Fleming (2015) suggests, makerspaces provide opportunities that encourage self-determination and entrepreneurship in our students. Often school makerspaces are open for student activity before school, during lunch or recess, and after school. In short, while they differ in goals and methodology, both STEM Labs and makerspaces offer valuable STEM learning experiences and can easily co-exist.

THE CONTRIBUTORS

Throughout the country numerous schools are already pursuing the vision of a digital age education through project-based learning in STEM Labs. Many of these schools are well documented and their leaders well known. For the purposes of this book, we chose individuals who work in schools that are not necessarily well known. These individuals could be any one of you. Roughly two dozen state, regional, district, and local school leaders were interviewed for this book, representing the perspectives of public and private schools at all levels and in urban, suburban, and rural settings. The unifying characteristic of all these contributors is their commitment to STEM education and belief in the value of STEM Labs. Their responses were illuminating and inspiring.

A STEP-BY-STEP GUIDE

Note that chapters of this book may be read sequentially; however, the business of building a STEM Lab may not always be a linear process. Recognizing that this volume may find its way into the hands of readers at different stages of STEM Lab implementation or differing needs, each chapter is freestanding. Further, in the limited parameters of this presentation, it is not possible to provide a fully comprehensive discussion of each topic. We hope that the ideas presented here can serve as a springboard for further conversation and investigation in your own district or school.

This what you can anticipate from the following chapters of this book:

CHAPTER 1: "Idea + Passion + Opportunity" describes the role of the leader in developing the STEM Lab. The ability to envision the end product, passionately recruit supporters, and take advantage of opportunities both within and outside of the school community reflects key attributes of a STEM Leadership mindset.

CHAPTER 2: "Preparing a Strong Foundation," explains the need for a strategic plan to help map your vision. Every successful building strategy requires a blueprint, and a STEM Lab is no exception. The strategic plan is also an important tool for enrolling stakeholders.

CHAPTER 3: "Building a Budget," offers critical information about how to create a budget and where to find budgetary resources. This is the moment for STEM education, and budget constraints should not be a barrier to success.

CHAPTER 4: "It Takes a Village," shares information about a variety of partnerships that can help support your STEM Lab. You don't have to do this alone. Local universities, businesses, and nonprofit organizations are great resources.

CHAPTER 5: "PD That Fits to a T (as in Technology)," presents a variety of practical approaches for training and engaging your faculty in the day-to-day work of the STEM Lab. Teachers are at the heart of the successful implementation of a STEM Lab.

CHAPTER 6: "At the Intersection of STEM Lab and Curriculum," frames STEM Lab activity in the context of national and state standards. STEM leaders weigh in on how to determine which projects are best for your STEM Lab.

CHAPTER 7: "Ready, Set . . . Now Implement," looks at the administrative challenges involved in running a STEM Lab and offers a few different approaches for the lab's oversight.

CHAPTER 8: "Impact and Expectations," focuses on the student as stakeholder in the building of a STEM Lab. Student voice and choice are addressed in a discussion of assessment in this context.

Quite a few books have been published that will explain how to set up a STEM Lab or makerspace, namely what kind of hardware, software, materials, tools, and machines you might want to include. We will reference some of these helpful books, but we don't intend to repeat their efforts. This book targets the needs of the school leader or technology coach from a macro perspective, that of an agent of change. We look to provide practical advice for the individuals who must first envision all of the pieces of the puzzle and then assemble them with the best chance for success.

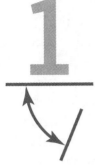

1 IDEA + PASSION + OPPORTUNITY

It's about having the persistence to keep at this work and to trust that—if you believe in what you are doing—you will be able to find allies and keep on building.

—TIKVAH WIENER,
FOUNDER AND PRINCIPAL, THE IDEA SCHOOL, TENAFLY, NEW JERSEY

DRIVING QUESTIONS

➤ Does it matter where the idea for a STEM Lab came from?

➤ What is a STEM Leadership mindset?

➤ What is the formula for success in establishing a STEM Lab?

TOP DOWN OR BOTTOM UP: DOES IT MATTER?

In some cases the idea to build a STEM Lab is part of a state, regional, or district mandate. In others, it is the result of organic programmatic growth within the school. There are still others who look to add a STEM Lab because it is the latest trend. Does the origin of the idea make a difference? Yes and no. It is always easier to implement change with the blessings and the budgetary support of the powers that be; it is not always a guarantee of success. Colleagues have shared unfortunate tales of moldering STEM Labs with equipment still in the original packaging or tucked away, unused in closets. The most important thing is not the origin of the idea, but its ownership. As Dr. Norma Fernandez, Director of the Discovery Division of Jersey City, New Jersey, describes it, you need to build consensus and to make sure that building leaders and faculty are fully engaged and committed. Aim for commitment rather than simply settling for compliance.

Many different types of stakeholders need to be involved in the process of building a STEM Lab. The teachers, however, are of particular importance. Although the idea for a STEM Lab may begin with the school, district leader, or leadership team, success is not possible without the support and dedication of the teachers who bring the STEM education and the STEM Lab to life.

STEM LEADERSHIP AS A MINDSET

Changing an entrenched system, with traditional expectations about classroom learning, is not easy. STEM leadership begins with a commitment to building a culture of transformative STEM teaching and learning, while providing opportunities and access for all students. For many schools STEM education, with its interdisciplinary, project-based methodology, represents a significant challenge because it introduces new tools, content, and methods of instruction. Transformative change requires transformational leadership. According to Northouse (2013), transformational leaders are individuals who have "a strong set of internal values and ideals" and are "effective at motivating followers" (p. 191). In other words, commitment and charisma are valuable tools for the leader who is facilitating change in what may be a resistant environment.

In the example of the A.D. Sullivan School, STEM transformation did not come about all at once. The impetus for growth came when Martha learned about the Latinas in STEM Foundation and attended one of their conferences at Stevens Institute of Technology. This foundation hosts conferences nationwide in an effort to educate girls in underserved communities and to encourage parents to support the educational growth of their children. Martha was inspired by what she observed and decided that it would be exciting to replicate the STEM 101 conference in the A.D. Sullivan School.

In March 2016, the school hosted its own STEM 101 conference with the sponsorship of the Latinas in STEM Foundation and with support from members of the Society of Hispanic Professional Engineers (SHPE) at Stevens Institute of Technology. This first of its kind event in Jersey City brought together nearly 200 participants, including representatives from local colleges and universities along with students, parents, teachers, volunteers, and local community members. The energy and excitement generated by this event encouraged Martha to begin looking for other STEM learning opportunities and potential partnerships for the school. Ultimately, this led to the idea of building a STEM Lab.

In the summer of 2016, the A.D. Sullivan School leadership team—which included the principal, the assistant principal, key faculty members, and the district science supervisor—met to discuss the possibility of a STEM Lab. Martha pushed hard for a designated space because she felt that it would extend STEM learning capacity within the school, provide opportunities to gather resources and tools to support STEM learning, and help her to enlist more STEM advocates by keeping a positive focus on STEM activity. The group developed a plan based on the needs of the students, curriculum, budget, resources, professional development, and logistics. In the fall of 2016, one of the classrooms was cleared, cleaned, and transformed into a STEM Lab. In the beginning, the school repurposed existing tables and chairs. Shortly after the lab was established, a local entrepreneur partnered with A.D. Sullivan in further development of the STEM Lab by providing 3D printers, a specially designed worktable, and an aquaponics setup. Professional development for the teachers and a multi-session 3D design and printing project for the students were also included in the package. At this point, use of the lab gradually increased as teachers trained on the use of the equipment and began incorporating STEM Lab use into their curricula and into after-school activities.

As the experience of the A.D. Sullivan school suggests, building a successful STEM Lab is a learning process for the school leaders, the faculty, and the students. The school leader and/or technology coach models the growth mindset, while encouraging others to learn. The teachers mirror this process with the students. It is interesting to note that the technological requirements of the STEM Lab are often a trigger for a somewhat more horizontal learning relationship between the student and the teacher. Chani Lichtiger, the STEM Coordinator at Yavneh Academy observes: "I have seen a shift where technology is concerned. More and more teachers are okay saying to the students: 'I don't know how to do this and I am going to learn with you.' There are even times when the students bring me advanced projects and they become my teachers."

ISTE STANDARD
CONNECTED LEARNER

Leaders model and promote continuous professional learning for themselves and others. Education leaders:

5d. Develop the skills needed to lead and navigate change, advance systems and promote a mindset of continuous improvement for how technology can improve learning.

Building a successful and effective STEM Lab is a challenge for all of the school's stakeholders. It is important for school leaders and technology coaches to model a growth mindset, showing their willingness to learn, while encouraging others to do so as well.

THE FORMULA FOR SUCCESS

Reflecting upon the process that led to the successful launch of the A.D. Sullivan STEM Lab, we decided that it can be summarized with a simple formula: **Idea + Passion + Opportunity.** Transformation begins with an idea: a visit to another school, attendance at a workshop, or reading articles about innovative STEM Labs. These experiences germinate until the idea emerges. The idea—considered, refined, and articulated—becomes the vision, and then the vision becomes the basis for the plan of action.

Next you need to find your passion. What is it that makes the idea exciting and inspirational? What will motivate you to sustain the effort that is required? Persistence is not enough. What is needed is passion. Passion is contagious and will inspire others. As Martha describes it: "The school leader sets the tone. I shared my excitement over every STEM accomplishment in the school. The faculty and students followed my lead."

The final piece of the formula is opportunity. "Opportunities" include partners, sources for funding, and different kinds of resources. With an open eye and a bit of effort, you can find opportunities everywhere. Dave Janosz sums up his experience by suggesting: "The best strategy that I found is to plug yourself into the business and industry networks. It's really up to you as an educator to make your own connections and to realize the value that [partners] can bring to your program." Contests, grants, and partnerships are examples of the kinds of opportunities that can energize your students and grow your STEM Lab (Figure 1.1).

FIGURE 1.1 Robot prototypes in the A.D. Sullivan STEM Lab.

STEM LAB STORY
THE IDEA SCHOOL, TENAFLY, NEW JERSEY

The name of the school featured in this vignette so irresistibly echoes the algorithm for a successful STEM Lab that it suggests we had no choice but to use it. Actually, the name was serendipitous. The motivation for this choice was the fact that The Idea School represents a very exciting educational approach with regard to STEM Labs. Instead of retrofitting an established school with ensconced methodologies to fit the needs of digital age education, The Idea School opened as a private high school in September 2018 and has embraced innovation from the ground up. The Idea School, which might be called an ideal school from a STEM perspective, is a project-based learning program focusing on interdisciplinary learning, design thinking, and the use of a carefully designed STEAM Lab, which they call a makerspace.

For Tikvah Wiener, the founder and head of The Idea School, the journey toward founding The Idea School began with a job as an English teacher. She moved from the classroom to a position in the school's administration, but she eventually left for the opportunity to work in a school dedicated to "project-based learning on a larger, curricular level." Tikvah began blogging about project-based learning and sharing her ideas and experiences with other educators. Shortly thereafter, she received a grant to fund the "Idea Schools Network," a program offering workshops in project-based learning. Subsequently, that program morphed into the Idea Institute, a platform for professional development in design thinking and STEAM education, as well as project-based learning.

Tikvah's passion for project-based and full-interdisciplinary learning inspired her to consider building a high school from scratch. She traveled to San Diego to visit High Tech High, a project-based learning high school founded by Larry Rosenstock in 2000. She has since returned to High Tech High numerous times for additional observation of their program and has participated in the High Tech High yearlong program in Graduate Education. In all, Rosenstock has been her mentor in the process of envisioning and developing The Idea School.

Tikvah gives several reasons for her decision to design the Idea School based on the model of High Tech High. The first is that High Tech High has completely set aside the factory model of education in favor of project-based learning. The students are engaged "in deep and meaningful learning," connecting what they study to the real world, and are encouraged to be "producers of content, products, and projects, and not mindless consumers" (The Idea School, 2018, para. 3). In addition, Tikvah shares Rosenstock's view that the project-based learning is a process of connecting head, hand, and heart. As such, it unifies the individual's thoughts with his/her actions and emotional connection to the activity of learning.

Tikvah's goal is to cultivate this ethos in The Idea School's STEAM-centric program, in which the students are encouraged to explore technology use not for its own sake, but as a means of improving people's lives. She explains: "In a unit on pursuing justice, we ask the students to choose a nonprofit that really speaks to them and to decide how are they going to make an impact. Well, let's say a student chooses a nonprofit with the mission of helping to get material care for an underserved population. The student may choose to prototype a product in the STEAM Lab to accomplish that goal. Another kid might decide to prepare a social media campaign, and another kid might decide to actually go volunteer for a certain number of hours per week." In this high school model, student voice and choice are driving factors.

"It is hard," Tikvah adds, "because the whole system is telling you that it's all about standardized testing. *You can't change things. It's much too difficult.* The whole system is telling you no, but you have to believe in what you are doing."

CHAPTER 1 RECAP

Envisioning and creating a successful STEM Lab requires a strong leader. In Chapter 1, we captured the essence of the STEM leadership mindset in the following points:

➤ The genesis of the idea to build a STEM Lab matters less than the leader's (or leaders') commitment to building a culture of transformative STEM teaching and learning, which provides opportunities and access for all students.

➤ In the process of building a successful STEM Lab, the school leaders, the faculty, and the students engage with challenges to the educational status quo. A growth mindset is needed to support this engagement with change.

➤ The formula for success is: idea + passion + opportunity. It requires a strong leader, who can envision the end product, passionately recruit supporters, and take advantage of opportunities both within and outside of the school community.

From the broad overview of the process presented in this chapter, our next step is to begin looking at the specific guideposts on the path to a STEM Lab. The journey begins with vision, the cornerstone of your project. Embedded in this step are the questions: What do we want to do, and how will we know if we have succeeded?

2

PREPARING A STRONG FOUNDATION

We needed our STEM facilities to basically match our course offerings and meet the needs of those curricular areas. Now our spaces say to the students, "Come in and learn how to use some of these tools and equipment. You can use them to design anything that you want."

**—DAVE JANOSZ,
SUPERVISOR, REGIONAL VALLEY HIGH SCHOOL, DEMAREST, NEW JERSEY**

DRIVING QUESTIONS

➤ What is the role of vision in building a STEM Lab?

➤ Who are the key stakeholders and how can they be enrolled as supporters?

➤ What is included in a strategic plan?

➤ How can you build in benchmarks for evaluation?

➤ What is the purpose of a timetable?

DEVELOPING A VISION

Vision is a crucial element in setting the expectations and future goals for a school building or district. Not only is it essential to have a vision for the school, it's equally important to have a clearly articulated vision when developing a STEM Lab. As Dave Janosz reminds us, a STEM Lab needs to align with the vision and goals of the school and the curriculum. At all points in planning and implementation of the lab, the vision will be the means of both guiding and measuring progress on an ongoing basis.

Each school and leadership team will develop its own vision, but looking at vision statements from institutions across the country, there are a few common themes:

➤ The vision reflects long-range thinking, looking beyond graduation to college and workforce readiness.

➤ The approach to STEM learning includes problem-based and inquiry-based methodologies. Frequently, design thinking is highlighted in the problem-solving process.

➤ Mention is made of rigorous content, where students are exposed to high-level ideas and information that is delivered in age-appropriate language.

➤ There is a focus on authenticity in the types of problems that are addressed in student work. Problems are also viewed in context and contrast to Big Questions or Powerful Ideas.

➤ The personal and social development of the student are primary objectives, where qualities of self-efficacy, resilience, empathy, and responsibility are highlighted along with communication, collaboration, and critical thinking skills.

As the colloquialism goes: "Toto, we're not in Kansas anymore." These themes indicate the recognition that the demands of the digital age learner cannot be met with learning methodologies of the previous generation. Real life consists of interdisciplinary experiences that require critical thinking and problem solving, as well as ethical judgment and social responsibility. The increasing adoption of STEM Labs in schools across the country is an indication of the shift in educational vision to meet this challenge.

As the ISTE Standard for a visionary planner suggests, the journey from idea to vision requires teamwork. This is true both because the resulting vision statement will be stronger and because shared vision development is a tool for engaging stakeholders.

Dr. Mark Silk, an Instructor of Organizational Management at Saint Peter's University, cautions, "It is important to be willing to tweak your vision based on the feedback of others. Don't just invite stakeholders to the table, but actually listen to what they have to say. As committed as you are to your vision, it may be necessary to modify it to get as many people on board as possible."

ISTE STANDARD
VISIONARY PLANNER

Leaders engage others in establishing a vision, strategic plan and ongoing evaluation cycle for transforming learning with technology. Education leaders:

2a. Engage education stakeholders in developing and adopting a shared vision for using technology to improve student success, informed by the learning sciences.

The shared vision is your compass. It guides each decision in the process of planning, implementing, and evaluating the success of the STEM Lab.

ENROLLING STAKEHOLDERS

Who are these stakeholders and why do you need them? A stakeholder is a person who: benefits from a project; has a direct role in designing and/or implementing it; has a share of legal or financial responsibility for it; has the financial, political, or social status or capacity to promote the project; and anyone else who has a stake in the project's short- or long-term success. In plain language, stakeholders include students, parents, administrators and other district or state school leaders, STEM coordinators and coaches, faculty, IT managers, custodial staff, the Board of Directors or School Board, potential funders, politicians, businesses, and community members. If we left anyone out, please fill in the blanks. The point here is that a STEM Lab, as a project with the potential to drive change, takes place in a larger context than simply the student-teacher relationship. If the results of this type of educational change are to be consequential, a lot of people need to be involved.

Let's begin with the faculty. As district leader Dr. Norma Fernandez told us: "The principal makes sure that funding is available, provides the support and the facilities, manages the finances, and so on. As the leader, you have the big picture, but you need others to do the day-to-day work." It is not over-stating the case to say that success rests with your faculty, but engaging the faculty is not always easy. Martha describes her feeling at the beginning of the project as something like the kind of leader that Derek Sivers calls "the lone nut" (Sivers, 2010). In his TedTalk, *How to Start a Movement,* Sivers depicts a leader with a new idea as someone who is received at arm's length, and viewed as separate from the community. "A leader needs the guts to stand out and be ridiculed," suggests Sivers. Although the lone individual begins the movement with little buy-in, a few followers can rapidly change the situation and catapult the movement forward.

This scenario describes Martha's experience while introducing the idea of project-based learning in a STEM Lab to her faculty. The initial reaction was mixed, as some of the teachers felt that the suggestion of a new methodology, the requirement to learn new technologies, and the idea of integrating previously separate subject matter was too much to consider. Happily, there were a few enthusiastic individuals who stepped forward in support of her vision. The initial stakeholders from within the faculty became the leaders of the initiative in practice within the school. Eventually, with the faculty working peer-to-peer in training one another and supporting the use of new technologies, she was able to encourage buy-in from the entire staff and to begin shifting the culture of the school.

Although other stakeholders may not play as immediate a role in building a STEM Lab, it is equally important to think about ways to engage them. At A.D. Sullivan, parents are invited to join the students in the STEM 101 Conference and in other related activities. At Yavneh Academy, school board members read and discussed articles about project-based learning and STEM. They attended hands-on workshops in the STEM Lab and visited other schools to learn about STEM Labs firsthand. Sometimes stakeholders can be addressed as a group, and at other times the school leader must simply present the case and build interest on a one-on-one basis.

Students are stakeholders too. We tend to consider them a blank canvas; eagerly awaiting whatever educational activity is planned for the day. The fact is that our students have the most skin in the game: It is their education and their future. While most react joyously as digital natives when given the opportunity to learn using technology and to engage in hands-on activity, there are also those who may resist change. "Why are you asking me to choose? Why don't you just tell me what I have to do?" is a response that is not as unusual as one might believe. Sometimes students need to be brought onboard just like their adult counterparts.

Imagine that at this point you have worked hard to engage all of your stakeholders, shared and shaped a mutually endorsed vision, and prepared and executed a plan. Is the work of enrolling stakeholders complete? Unfortunately, no.

A new superintendent takes office, the principal retires, your STEM coach moves to a different district, teachers are replaced, and in the natural course of things, students graduate. Cultivating interest and engagement in the vision and enrollment of stakeholders is an ongoing commitment.

ISTE STANDARD
VISIONARY PLANNER

Leaders engage others in establishing a vision, strategic plan and ongoing evaluation cycle for transforming learning with technology. Education leaders:

2b. Build on the shared vision by collaboratively creating a strategic plan that articulates how technology will be used to enhance learning.

The strategic plan is not only a road map to success; it is also an important tool for engaging stakeholders with a shared vision and concrete expectations for action.

PLANNING YOUR WORK AND WORKING YOUR PLAN

Once you have established a shared vision and have the support of the stakeholders, you can begin developing a strategic plan. Most education leaders, by the time they reach that level of responsibility have already experienced the strategic planning process. For those less familiar, there are countless books and articles that can suggest a framework. For the purposes of strategic planning in the context of building a STEM Lab, we will offer only a few helpful hints that we feel are relevant:

➤ **BEGIN BY TAKING AN INVENTORY.** The traditional approach to strategic plan often includes the S.W.O.T. (or Strengths, Weaknesses, Opportunities, and Threats) analysis for barriers and facilitators of success. Before you begin, it is important to take an honest look at the school program and resources. This will help you establish a baseline for your goals and benchmarks. As well, you may find that you have more capacity to build a STEM Lab than you at first imagined.

➤ **KEEP IT SIMPLE.** Reeves (2008) suggests that a one-page plan is far more effective and manageable than the classic approach of generating a lengthy and detailed document. He uses the example of the *Plan on a Page* (Freeport School District, 2007) as a useable strategic planning tool. Only four areas are addressed by the plan: "student performance, human resources, partnerships, and equity. For each of these key areas, the plan lists two to five goals and measures. Each goal includes a clear statement of actions to accomplish" (Reeves, 2008, para. 13). One of the advantages of this type of strategic plan is its accessibility. It is easy to use in periodic spot checks of progress and for discussions at leadership team or board meetings.

➤ **USE S.M.A.R.T. GOALS.** S.M.A.R.T. goals (Figure 2.1) are a favorite tool for many administrators because they offer yet another simple and straightforward method of planning. First introduced by George T. Doran (1981), S.M.A.R.T. is an acronym for the characteristics of five goals: Specific, Measurable, Assignable, Realistic, and Time-related.

S.M.A.R.T. GOALS

S—SPECIFIC

➤ What are the long- and short-term goals?

➤ What are the desired outcomes?

➤ What resources (including funding) are available?

M—MEASUREABLE

➤ How can success be measured?

➤ What are the benchmarks for evaluation?

A—ASSIGNABLE

➤ Who will be the key stakeholders assigned to each task?

R—REALISTIC

➤ What results can be achieved within the given timeframe and resources?

T—TIME-RELATED

➤ When will these results be achieved?

➤ By when do I expect the desired outcome?

(Doran, 1981)

FIGURE 2.1 S.M.A.R.T. goals allow you to generate a plan by simply answering a series of questions, as shown here.

STEM LAB STORY
NORTHERN VALLEY REGIONAL HIGH SCHOOL, DEMAREST, NEW JERSEY

Dave Janosz would readily agree that planning and building two STEM Labs in each of his district's two high schools takes time—roughly four years in this case. Dave is the Supervisor of Technology and Engineering for Northern Valley Regional High School and the Supervisor of Instructional Technology for the district. He led the effort to renovate the schools' former shop facilities to create STEM Labs. According to Dave, two of these are more "heavy-duty" facilities called the "STEM Fabrication Labs" and the others are design and prototyping facilities called "STEM Design Labs."

Dave explains his vision: "I wanted to design a facility that matches a modern STEM and Maker mindset. More importantly, I wanted it to facilitate project- and problem-based learning. You don't get the sense that you can accomplish those things when you walk into a classroom that's set up with rows of chairs." By contrast, the STEM Labs have heavy-duty mobile tables, topped with thick butcher block material. The tables' height is 36 inches so that students can choose to stand or sit in tall stools with seatbacks (Figure 2.2).

FIGURE 2.2 STEM Design Lab at Northern Valley Regional High School.

Northern Valley Regional High Schools now have the use of four outstanding STEM Labs. Dave began planning these facilities around 2012, and they were operational in 2016 (Figures 2.3 and 2.4). Dave attributes the length of the process to three factors, none of them related to the actual building of the spaces and the acquisition of furniture and equipment. The first reason was the curriculum. Dave and his colleagues have spent the past four or five years creating new program pathways for students who wish to study engineering, computer science, and bioengineering. The goal of the STEM Labs is to support the course offerings; therefore, the curriculum development needed to come first.

FIGURE 2.3 The space was designed for increased flexibility, with movable furniture and storage units.

FIGURE 2.4 The space also offers tool accessibility, with visible tool storage.

The second reason it took several years was funding. The funding for these STEM Labs was obtained through a public referendum. The towns in this region voted to allocate their tax dollars for this purpose. Political process takes time, although in this case patience and perseverance were well rewarded. The third reason was enrollment of stakeholders. Dave was the passionate trailblazer in this instance. "It took a lot of time to basically talk it up to the principals, the business office, the superintendent, and the buildings and grounds committee. I didn't encounter a lot of resistance. In fact, I found a lot of support, especially from the district's business administrator and the two building principals."

Dave is very satisfied with the progress of the STEM programs since opening the labs. "We frequently partner with the Science and Math departments, and have had teachers from other departments take an interest in what's going on. We have created a buzz in the schools because educators of all backgrounds understand that STEM is going to be at the core of a lot of students' future careers and interests. They understand that project-based learning is important; and they see that in the courses we teach in this department, that's where the teachers have the time, knowledge, and capacity to deliver project-based learning in a meaningful way."

MEASURING SUCCESS

Evaluation of the STEM Lab begins during the planning process. By setting action goals, or S.M.A.R.T. goals, you are establishing the benchmarks that will be used to measure success. The *Plan on a Page* (Freeport School District, 2007) described above identifies four areas for evaluation. Regarding the STEM Lab, a fifth category might be considered; that is the physical plant and equipment. Particularly in the early stages of development, it will be helpful to determine whether the environment is effectively configured and if the available tools are meeting your needs.

Of course, student assessments and feedback are going to provide the most important measures of success. Grading rubrics align the assessment with the performance goals for students, while portfolios of student work and presentations provide the tangible representations of achievement. We will expand upon this topic in the discussion of student voice and choice in Chapter 8, "Impact and Expectations."

In terms of the overall evaluation process, it is important to monitor progress and perform periodic, thoughtful evaluations and assessments. No later than six months into the process, an appropriate evaluation will both provide direction for course corrections and information that can be shared with key stakeholders. Remember to celebrate your successes—it is a great way to build goodwill.

ISTE STANDARD
VISIONARY PLANNER

Leaders engage others in establishing a vision, strategic plan and ongoing evaluation cycle for transforming learning with technology. Education leaders:

2c. Evaluate progress on the strategic plan, make course corrections, measure impact and scale effective approaches for using technology to transform learning.

2d. Communicate effectively with stakeholders to gather input on the plan, celebrate successes and engage in a continuous improvement cycle.

The collective power of the stakeholders can serve as an immense driving force when developing the strategic plan. Within the team, there should be one or more members with expertise in technology and the digital learner.

IT'S ABOUT TIME

The good thing about time is that it is measurable and unambiguous. The challenging thing about time is that sometimes—particularly when you are building out a new space or even a new program—timing can only be a best guess. So why bother with a timetable? The timetable is useful because it provides mutually agreed upon targets for completion. Generally, it is a tool for the management of planning and implementation. When the timetable is met, it is cause for satisfaction. When it is not, there is an opportunity for reflection on possibilities for improvement.

CHAPTER 2 RECAP

Every successful building strategy requires a blueprint and a STEM Lab is no exception. A strategic plan helps map your vision and is an important tool for enrolling stakeholders. In the vision development process, it is important to remember:

➤ A clear vision frames stakeholder expectations for your STEM Lab. The vision for the STEM Lab must also align with that of the school and curriculum.

➤ Planning and building a STEM Lab requires teamwork. School leaders, teachers, staff, students, parents, and partners are all needed to create and sustain the lab.

➤ The strategic plan should include S.M.A.R.T. goals and objectives, benchmarks for success and an evaluation plan, a budget, and a timetable for implementation.

With an overall plan in hand, attention now turns to realizing each individual step. One of the first steps is to put funding in place. The next chapter discusses the particulars of budgeting for a STEM Lab and recommends sources for funding.

BUILDING A BUDGET

I think as long as we can demonstrate value, which is relatively easy to do, then the funding will be there.

—STEVE FREEDMAN,
HEAD OF SCHOOL, HILLEL DAY SCHOOL OF METROPOLITAN DETROIT

DRIVING QUESTIONS

➤ Should budget drive the decision to build a STEM Lab?

➤ What are the considerations in building a budget for a STEM Lab?

➤ Where can my school find funding for a STEM Lab?

BUDGET BASICS

Budget is, of course, a pivotal element in planning a STEM Lab. It is also one of the most frequently cited barriers to building a STEM Lab. For that reason, we felt that the discussion of budget merits its own chapter. It is rare to find a school without some budget limitations. Urban and rural schools, in particular, are known to have extreme financial challenges. Is budget really the showstopper when it comes to building a STEM Lab? With full respect to the economic challenges facing education, we suggest that it need not be. There are many different approaches to establishing a STEM Lab, ranging from repurposing available space and furniture to demolishing whole sections of your school and building from scratch. A STEM Lab can begin with a moveable cart or a designated area of classrooms and grow over time. Budget-wise, it is not a one-size-fits-all proposition.

"We didn't have any outside funding when we started the STEM Lab, just our school budget," said Dr. Janet Elder, Principal at the Christa McAuliffe School (interview, May 15, 2018). At the Christa McAuliffe School, the STEM Lab began with the repurposing of a large room that was used for storage and supplies. The administration, faculty, parent volunteers, and custodial staff pitched in to transform the room into a functional and inviting space for hands-on learning (Figure 3.1).

FIGURE 3.1 Students at the Christa McAuliffe School engaged in work in the STEM Lab.

There is no question that building a STEM Lab requires effort and funding. For some schools it is a matter of reallocation of resources. It may take the form of sweat equity, as in the example above. It may require navigating political byways to get the benefit of a special allocation. It may be a matter of grant writing or a bit of extra hustle to find a donor. Or it may be a combination of the above. Our point is that it is important not to give up before you investigate the possibilities. Marcos Navas, Technology Coordinator for the Union City Public Schools, suggests the initial effort is a good investment: "Once the administration, teachers, and students see the positive value of the work in the STEM Lab and the value of the tools that you are investing in, it just becomes a part of the budget and ecosystem."

BUDGET CONSIDERATIONS

As with the rest of the STEM Lab plan, your vision and goals drive the budget.

The types of tools and furniture that can be used in a STEM Lab vary widely. Choices, and therefore line items in your budget, should depend upon the answers to the questions: How will we use this, and how will it help to fulfill our goals for student learning? Research is the best tool for making and budgeting for design choices. In addition to consulting books and articles about designing STEM Labs and makerspaces, it is helpful to visit other schools that have already established labs.

The financial resources of the STEM Labs described in this book range from shoestring to multi-millions. Wherever you are on this spectrum, we'd like to share a piece of common sense advice that we received from multiple contributors: Make sure to check your storage closets. You may find useful machines or equipment that someone may have ordered and forgotten about. Especially if you plan to include a STEAM or makerspace area in the lab, unused craft materials can be put to good use.

Along with curricular goals, equity and inclusion are important considerations. Dr. Patricia Holzman, the Director of the STEM Resource Lab at the A. Harry Moore School, Jersey City, New Jersey, suggests that the crux of inclusion "is all about knowing your student population and planning for their needs. The same physical and technological accommodations that you make in every other part of the school will also need to be present in the STEM Lab."

In many communities, the digital divide is a reality. Kirk Brown is the Technology Director for the San Joaquin Valley Region in California. Within this region are very populated, urban areas and single-school districts. Kirk describes one of the functions of their regional STEM Lab as accommodating the needs of students who live in migrant camps or areas. They serve a number of migrant communities, with a large proportion of English language learners. These are students who have limited access to technology at home. Also, when they are out of school, there is not a lot for them to do. The STEM Lab hosts them in summer camps for coding and microscopy.

ISTE STANDARD
EQUITY AND CITIZENSHIP ADVOCATE

Leaders use technology to increase equity, inclusion, and digital citizenship practices. Education leaders:

1b. Ensure all students have access to the technology and connectivity necessary to participate in authentic and engaging learning opportunities.

Effective leaders understand the needs of their student population and plan accordingly to eliminate the digital divide and barriers to success. This includes creating an inclusive setting where students have the same physical and technical accommodations that exist within other parts of the school building.

DESIGN CONSIDERATIONS

The STEM Lab is an opportunity to provide the students with an aesthetically inviting and comfortable space for their problem-solving activities. Here are a few of the design considerations with regard to the physical plan for the STEM Lab.

FLEXIBILITY

Mobile workstations and moveable chairs make it possible to easily reconfigure the room for different uses. Tables come in all shapes and sizes, effectively enabling small work groups, as well as larger demonstration lessons. Variable height and surface materials for the tables address other needs. Movable room dividers provide a space that can be subdivided for simultaneous use with group work, lectures, and individual computer research.

SEATING

Moveable stools with seat backs, soft stools, mats that can be used for sitting on the floor, and seating nooks are examples of the types of seating that accommodate the varied needs of learning in the STEM Lab.

COMPUTER HARDWARE AND EQUIPMENT

Perimeter workstations, laptop or tablet carts, and tables with interface tops are typically found in STEM Labs, particularly in those with a design focus. Charging stations for electronic devices are also a helpful addition.

Different types of equipment and materials require different kinds of work areas. For example, computers, electronics, soldering, and small hand tool areas are most often found in a stationary, perimeter workstation. Similarly, 3D printers, laser-cutting machines, saws, and metal working tools require a permanent location in a less crowded part of the lab. There are a few different options for the electrical outlets that support mobile workspaces. Some schools install floor outlets that can be covered when the furniture is moved to another part of the room. Other schools create a system of extension cords that are suspended from the ceiling and can be retracted when not in use.

STORAGE AND SECURITY

Two types of storage are needed for STEM Labs. Materials, portable equipment, and small tools must be organized and accessible. Student also need a place to store their work in progress. The amount of space will depend on the size of student projects and the types of material involved.

Locking cabinets, computer carts, and, of course, a lock on the door to the room are a necessity. Taking an inventory of the assets in the lab is highly recommended and it serves multiple purposes. First and foremost, it is essential to keep track of valuable equipment including laptops, printers, and expensive machinery. Secondly, by having a clear understanding of the available assets, you will know whether additional items will need to be ordered. It is also ideal to record the vendor and model number of the key pieces of equipment. This will also make it easier when ordering parts or a replacement.

LOCATION

STEM Labs come in all shapes and sizes, depending on the needs and capacity of the school. When selecting a location, it is important to make sure that the space is either well ventilated or air-conditioned. Equipment and electrical devices can get overheated, and you want to ensure that the appropriate room temperature can be maintained. Rifkie Silverman, Chair of the Engineering and Computer Science Department at The Frisch School, Paramus, New Jersey, suggests that the STEM Lab should have a prominent position in the school. She recommends that it be a kind of fishbowl, completely open for observation by the entire school population. Accordingly, an entire wall of her school's STEM Lab is filled with windows opening into a well-trafficked hallway. The visibility of STEM Lab contributes to the energy and excitement around project-based learning.

INFRASTRUCTURE

David Rackliff, the IT Manager for the Emek School in Los Angeles, California, remembers attending an early planning where the school's leaders were introducing the idea of converting the school library into a STEM Lab. In the course of the discussion they asked him: "From a technology standpoint, what will we need to do in this space?" His reply: "That all depends upon what you want to do and what is required for the machines you plan to use in the lab" (private conversation, June 18, 2018). With help from a designer, this school produced an architectural drawing that showed the placement of computer stations on the perimeter, mobile workstations, seating areas, and a 60-inch monitor for video conferences and sharing design processes as well as student work.

Safety is an issue that needs to be considered when building a STEM Lab. David notes that the 3D printers, which did require 220V outlets and an upgrade for the school's electrical panel, also needed a space that could be vented so that the students didn't inhale fumes. Faculty and students should be trained on the proper use of the equipment, to protect the users and the school's investment.

PERSONNEL AND PROFESSIONAL DEVELOPMENT

Because STEM Labs vary so widely in their shape, size, and purpose, there are no generalizable recommendations with regard to staff. The 7000-square-foot regional STEM Lab serving San Joaquin Valley public schools has two full-time and two part-time staff members. Additional help is brought in on an as-needed basis. Yavneh Academy, which is less than one-third their size, has a staff comprised of the Technology Director and three teachers. Depending on how your school operates, personnel salaries may also be a part of your budget. For those who are just in the beginning stages of building a STEM Lab, you can take heart from the example of the A.D. Sullivan school. There Martha recruited the math coach as the organizer. This individual provided support as one of the peer trainers for the faculty.

Keep in mind the cost of the professional development needed to prepare your teachers for working in the lab. Sometimes it is possible to include this cost in requests for grant funding, or to train a few teachers who then work as peer coaches within the school. Conference participation, while a valuable investment, can be costly.

ISTE STANDARD
SYSTEM DESIGNER

Leaders build teams and systems to implement, sustain and continually improve the use of technology to support learning. Education leaders:

4b. Ensure that resources for supporting the effective use of technology for learning are sufficient and scalable to meet future demand.

When building a STEM Lab, design a system that is sustainable and will evolve with the needs of digital learners.

STEM LAB STORY
HILLEL DAY SCHOOL, FARMINGTON HILLS, MICHIGAN

The STEM Lab at the Hillel Day School is something of a Cinderella story (Figures 3.2 through 3.4).

When principal Steve Freedman first arrived at the K–8 school 15 years ago, he found an established institution where workbooks, seatwork, and lectures were the norm. The seed of a new vision for the school developed from the question: What would it take to transform the Hillel Day School into a school where meaningful and authentic learning was taking place?

Over the next decade, Steve worked with the faculty to cultivate a new vision for the school based on best practices in education. When that vision was captured on paper, it was clear that learning spaces needed to look very different to support a more creative and hands-on approach to learning (private communication, 2016). He then took the vision to the Board of Trustees. Multiple presentations for these school leaders eventually earned their support of the innovative vision. Board members accompanied Steve to a meeting with a local foundation and helped to win their support for upgrading the school's technology infrastructure as a first step toward their larger goal.

FIGURE 3.2 Small class sizes facilitate meaningful conferencing between teacher and student, allowing the differentiation that responds to a student's individual needs and interests.

The Cinderella moment came when a family philanthropist with connections to the school heard about the changes in the school and asked the school leaders a fateful question: "What transformative dream do you have for Hillel Day School?" As Steve describes that moment: "With our vision, story, and data in hand, we presented the donor with a master plan to transform the school into a 21st century learning center."

The foundation awarded the school a multi-million dollar grant, which enabled a full renovation of both the building and the curriculum. Now, at the heart of a completely re-configured layout is the school's innovation hub. It is a hive of interconnected spaces, where one enters through the library, continues through a teacher planning area into the prototyping lab, which connects to the makerspace and an arts studio.

FIGURE 3.3 Why stop to search for paper and pen when a writeable table sparks ideas and creativity that can be captured in the moment?

FIGURE 3.4 Small manipulatives and group work teach skills and concepts that set up our students for success in the world they will inherit.

These rooms then open into an open area with student workspace and finally into a greenhouse. As Steve explained, this STEAM-centered lab complex sends a message to the students that the school is a flexible, comfortable environment, where learning is our top priority and is also fun and child centered (private communication, 2016). The students use the space as a makerspace before and after school, as well as during recess. The teachers use it as a STEM Lab and a tool for interdisciplinary study.

The entire faculty has trained extensively in project-based learning. They work with the director of curriculum and the STEM Lab staff to plan their use of the space. Steve shared an example of the school's project-based, interdisciplinary approach that relates to another fairytale: Jack and the Beanstalk. First-grade students read the story, then "learn about soil, how things grow, and plant their own bean stalks in the greenhouse."

Steve describes the school's transformation in the past few years as a "long journey to understanding what are the needs of kids today and how do we get there? A lot of research, thinking, deliberation, visioning, and professional development took place before we actually did it" (interview, 2018). Perhaps the donor's gift was the stuff of fairytales, but the reality of creating a STEAM-Lab-centered school, Steve attributes to hard work, "a laser-focused approach, staying on message, and doggedly persevering leadership" (private communication, 2016).

BUILDING RESOURCES FOR YOUR STEM LAB

For those of you readers who have not yet built a STEM Lab, we know that you must be thinking: "All of this sounds great, but how can we fund it?" If you are lucky enough to be the New Hope School District in Thornton, California—a one-school district with only 200 students—you might take advantage of the state's local control account-ability plan that allows schools to decide how their budget will be allocated. For most of you, the bulk of the investment in a STEM Lab will be extra-budgetary. Here are a few ideas that were gathered from among the contributors to this book:

➤ Grants are available from both government and private foundation sources. You can apply for grants on behalf of your school or benefit from grants received by other institutions. Often universities and other institutions receive grants and need to find students to participate in their research or program offerings.

➤ STEM competitions are another potential source of funds for STEM Labs. The A. D. Sullivan School won valuable Science Buddy Kits in a competition sponsored by the Allergan Corporation. The Christa McAuliffe School won a $30,000 cash prize in the Lexus Challenge. These are examples of urban elementary schools. Similar opportunities are available for high schools.

➤ Donations from private individuals and businesses are another way to fund STEM Lab creation and acquisition of equipment and furniture. In addition, there may be parents who are employed by corporations that may be willing to support your efforts. Public schools, in particular, need to make sure that they follow district poli-cies and regulations when accepting gifts from the private sector.

➤ Crowdfunding, using internet sites such as GoFundMe and DonorsChoose, is another option.

➤ Parent Teacher Organization fundraisers are both a way to raise some funds and to educate and engage parents as stakeholders in the STEM Lab.

CHAPTER 3 RECAP

A limited budget should not be the determining factor in the decision to build a STEM Lab. If you have a limited budget, you can begin on a smaller scale and expand when more funds become available. There are many sources and resources that can help you achieve your goals. The key points in this chapter are as follows:

➤ Research is the best tool for making and budgeting for design choices.

➤ Remember that professional development is pivotal, and look for ways to support it within your budget.

➤ Know your student population, and plan for their needs. The same physical and technological accommodations that you make in every other part of the school will also need to be present in the STEM Lab.

➤ There are many different sources for funding beyond your existing budget. These include donations, grants, STEM competitions, crowdfunding, corporate gifts, and PTO fundraisers.

The main message regarding funding is to both carefully consider existing resources and be prepared to think outside of the box. Chapter 4 expands on this theme by discussing the value and potential contributions of community partners and other partnerships.

4

IT TAKES A VILLAGE

A lot of rural schools say that they don't have the resources for STEM partnerships. We encourage them to look at entrepreneurs and small businesses in their area. We have a couple of schools that have connected with nearby universities.

—MEGHAN MCFERRIN,
DOE STEM/STEAM PROGRAM SPECIALIST, ATLANTA, GEORGIA

DRIVING QUESTIONS

➤ What is the role of partnerships in building a STEM Lab?

➤ Where can partnerships be found?

➤ How do you know if the partnership is a good fit?

➤ What can parents contribute to your STEM Lab?

PARTNERSHIPS AND THE STEM LAB

In Chapter 1 we presented a formula for successfully building a STEM Lab that included developing ideas, fueling your passion, and searching for opportunities. The opportunities that we are referring to are partnerships within and outside of your community. With a focused vision in mind, begin to network and to develop your radar for potential STEM Lab resources in the form of partnerships.

A partnership is a mutually beneficial relationship, wherein each side contributes something and benefits in a particular way. Some partnerships are a source for equipment and materials, teacher training, or programs and activities for students. Partnerships can also be a source for funding. When the funder and the school share a common vision, the funder has an advisory role, and the funder is looking for a sustained relationship, it is more likely to create a partnership, or even a sponsorship, than a simple donor-and-recipient connection.

What are the strategic benefits of partnerships? First, a partnership with a respected organization and institution reinforces the value of your vision to your stakeholders. It sends the message that your school is not alone in its quest for transformational education. Second, your partner may be able to supply mentors, speakers, volunteers, or even the imprinted swag that adds to the success of a single school-wide STEM event or ongoing programs. Finally, a trusted partnership may provide you with opportunities to take advantage of particular kinds of business expertise (Figure 4.1). For example, the UA Maker Academy, a career technical education high school, has representatives from the design industry on its advisory board, and professionals from that industry serve as mentors for students.

FIGURE 4.1 Examples of the STEM Lab Partners at A.D. Sullivan include the Latinas in STEM, Liberty Science Center, Society of Hispanic Professional Engineers, and PicoTurbine.

ISTE STANDARD
SYSTEMS DESIGNER

Leaders build teams and systems to implement, sustain and continually improve the use of technology to support learning. Education leaders:

5d. Establish partnerships that support the strategic vision, achieve learning priorities and improve operations.

Partnerships with local science centers, colleges, universities, local government, and community businesses can provide STEM expertise, grants, professional development, and many other resources for your STEM Lab.

FINDING PARTNERS

Martha describes finding partners as her superpower, suggesting that within five minutes of conversation with a stranger she can ferret out partnership opportunities. Happily, finding partners is a superpower that anyone can cultivate by focusing on a few key steps:

➤ Listen carefully when people introduce themselves and ask questions about their work and area of expertise.

➤ Make your message portable. Refine your vision and goals into an "elevator speech" that can be presented in under a minute.

➤ Let your passion shine through. Positive energy sells the message.

➤ Look for the win-win. Partnerships are about mutual benefit. You know what you need for your STEM Lab, but what can a partner receive in return? Possible answers include access to a student target group, community service opportunities, a place to donate used or no longer needed equipment, and attention to a pipeline for future employees.

➤ Be flexible. Ask whether the business or organization has had experience partnering with schools? Would they be interested?

➤ Follow through. Frequently the initial conversation is a brief one. Make sure to share contact information and then to reach out in a follow-up email, text, or telephone call, depending on the nature of the connection.

In truth, finding partners is not really about random encounters. It is important to put yourself in places where you can encounter potential partners. This section will describe different sources for partnerships and where to find them.

LOCAL BUSINESSES AND INDUSTRY

You don't have to look too far to find businesses that can support your STEM Lab. STEM fields are growing and businesses are looking for a robust pipeline for future workers. Here are a few resources that can help with your search:

➤ Research your state Department of Education. Does it have a STEM Forum or another framework for connecting schools with businesses and industry?

➤ Check with your local Chamber of Commerce.

➤ Connect with business or industry networks or trade associations.

Dave Janosz, Supervisor of the Technology and Engineering Department of a public high school, recommends this practical approach:

> *The best strategy that I found, as an educator, is to try to plug yourself in. You can't expect business and industry to come to you offering their advice. Some large corporations might have STEM Outreach Programs, but most small or mid-sized companies don't have that kind of capacity. It's really up to you to make your own connections and recognize the value that business and industry can bring to your program. In my district we're not going to business and industry to fund our programs. We're going because we understand that they have something to say and they have good advice to give on our program development. They ask us: What's included in your program? Are the students writing? Are they doing technical writing? Are they researching? What are the projects that the students are working on? What are the skills that they're learning throughout the program? That is the value that business partners bring.*

For example, the A.D. Sullivan School launched their STEM Lab with the help of a local business. The science supervisor introduced Martha to the owner of PicoTurbine, a tech startup company in the community. PicoTurbine wanted to develop clientele that would call upon their business as a provider of STEM programs and professional development. Their goal was to build connections in the local district by working with a cohort of schools. With funding from the district, PicoTurbine provided teachers and students at A.D. Sullivan hands-on training in Tinkercad and 3D printing.

Because of this initial connection, PicoTurbine also became involved in building the STEM Lab. Personnel from PicoTurbine helped the school leaders design and organize the STEM Lab. PicoTurbine donated two custom-designed maker tables, installed shelving units to hold the 3D printers, created a dry erase board for one wall of the room, and donated a hydroponic station for the lab. The conclusion: Business partnerships can grow in unexpected directions.

UNIVERSITIES AND COLLEGES

Universities and colleges are excellent candidates for partnerships in STEM education and in your STEM Lab. Here are a few ways to connect with universities and colleges:

➤ Research STEM Education, Educational Technology, and other related departments in local universities, colleges, and community colleges. Introduce yourself to the director of the department and express that you are interested in having the university do research in STEM education in your school. (Note: Research proposals need to be approved by the Institutional Review Board of the university and, in the case of public schools, by school leaders and the Board of Education.)

➤ Find out if the higher education institutions have outreach projects for local schools and get your name on the mailing list.

➤ Find out if the higher education institution recommends or requires that their students get involved in community advocacy or service projects in their field of study; make friends with the campus coordinator for these activities.

➤ Look into the honor societies, fraternities, and sororities that may be looking for volunteer projects.

Higher education is a rich resource for partnerships because its leaders care about STEM education for the same reasons that we do; they are involved in grant-funded educational research and need access to K–12 students as study subjects; and most universities encourage both the students and the faculty to volunteer for community service projects. These institutions are also home to honor societies and other organizations that might be a fruitful source for volunteers. The first step in creating these partnerships is to reach out and introduce yourself.

For example, the Stevens Institute of Technology in Hoboken, New Jersey, and the New Jersey Institute of Technology (NJIT) in Newark, New Jersey, both offer a variety of workshops that are open to the community. These programs are provided by student societies and organizations within the college or university. Student chapters of the Society of Hispanic Professional Engineers (SHPE) are an example of organizations that offer special events and programming at these academic institutions. The goal of these programs is to expose middle and high school students to the various fields of engineering, such as civil engineering, mechanical engineering, computer engineering, and chemical engineering. At SHPE-sponsored events, students learn about the science of making ice cream, coding, and building structural designs using design thinking. These types of partnerships can pique the interest of students and expose them to potential STEM majors at an earlier age.

Campus organizations such as SHPE provide a bridge between K–12 education and higher education by exposing K–12 students to local colleges and universities and by offering STEM role models for younger students. Some of these organizations have K–12 outreach programs and support a local K–12 chapter. A.D. Sullivan is one of the schools with a SHPE junior chapter. Members of the SHPE Executive Board at NJIT visit the school and meet bi-weekly with the SHPE junior chapter members. The young learners are exposed to design thinking and STEM challenges, and they have the opportunity to learn from college students.

There are professional organizations for individuals in the STEM workforce that also offer programs for K–12 students. For example, Ruby Romero, a member of the SHPE New Jersey Professionals, works for Turner Construction. In February 2018, Ruby reached out to the school leadership team at A.D. Sullivan School to propose an event aimed at exposing young girls to engineering. Turner Construction sponsored the program, in which several female STEM professionals facilitated an engineering design challenge for the girls, followed by a panel discussion.

NONPROFIT ORGANIZATIONS, SCIENCE MUSEUMS, COMMUNITY AND LIBRARY MAKERSPACES

Nonprofit organizations, science museums, museums with makerspaces, and community and library makerspaces are potential partners, because they can help to enrich the STEM culture in the school and support the work in your STEM Lab. They can be a source of grants, off-site programs for students and parents, ideas, and personnel. Here are a few ways to identify prospective partners in your community:

➤ Research local resources online.

➤ Reach out and introduce yourself, and ask to be put on the mailing list of local organizations.

➤ Attend and volunteer your support for community events—these are great networking opportunities.

For example, the Latinas in STEM Foundation is a national, nonprofit organization whose mission is to encourage middle- and high-school-aged girls to pursue careers in STEM fields. This organization provides workshops for students and parents in underserved communities, with the ultimate goal of increasing the number of Latina women pursuing STEM careers and creating a network to support women in STEM. Girls Who Code is another example of a national nonprofit organization with the mission of encouraging girls to excel in STEM. Girls Who Code offers free after-school clubs for girls in Grades 3–12. This organization will also lend support to local STEM conferences, such as the annual Girls in Technology Symposium sponsored by Hudson County Community College, in Jersey City, New Jersey.

The Liberty Science Center (LSC) is a science museum and learning center located in Jersey City, New Jersey. The LSC applies for grants to support educational outreach programs in the community. Under a grant from the Clare Foundation, students in early childhood participate in hands-on exploration with experts from LSC during the course of three years. The services provided through this grant follow the students from year to year, beginning in prekindergarten and ending in Grade 1. The funding provides teachers with an opportunity to engage in professional development with experts in the field. The grant also includes admission for the school community, including the parents, to visit the science center.

A community makerspace is a workshop or lab supported by its membership. There are approximately 500 such makerspaces in the United States (Lou & Peek, 2016). Community makerspaces are also potential partners for school-based STEM Labs. The San Joaquin County Office of Education Fab Lab, a regional school STEM Lab, partners with the community Fab Lab in Stockton, California. These two labs share equipment and expertise, and welcome visitors from each other's catchment area. The Bergen County Makerspace in Hackensack, New Jersey, offers professional development programs and workshops for the area's teachers.

The Idea School high school is located in the education wing of a Jewish Community Center (JCC). Various groups use the building, including a preschool, a special needs program, and a senior adult community. In partnership with the JCC, the Idea School offers use of the school's STEM Lab "as a multigenerational makerspace" and invites participation from all of the resident communities.

TRYING PARTNERSHIPS ON FOR SIZE

A partnership is a purposeful relationship between people or organizations that reflects a commitment to a common goal. There are many different kinds of partnerships. The guidelines for productive partnerships may not be the same in every case. For example, in a long-term partnership, planning together at the outset is a good investment of time. A school that rents space from another organization or plans to share its STEM Lab with the larger community is an example of a long-term partnership. In a short-term partnership, such as a one-time event or a limited grant-funded program, getting to know the organization and engaging in strategic planning is not realistic. With this in mind, there are several generally accepted principles that can help you effectively navigate partnerships:

➤ **SHARED VISION:** Every decision and action that you take in building a STEM Lab should be measured with the yardstick of your vision. Partnerships are no exception. The purpose of a partnership is to help you achieve specific goals. So at the outset you need to ask: How will this partnership help us achieve our goals?

➤ **CLEAR ROLES AND RESPONSIBILITIES:** Make sure that expectations are clearly stated. The culture of a school is very different from that of other kinds of businesses and organizations. Partners will need to understand that they do not have full autonomy when working with students, either on- or off-campus. They must abide by the established policies and rules of the school.

➤ **MUTUALLY ACCEPTABLE GROUND RULES:** In addition to creating an understanding about in what form and how often communications between the partners should take place, establish a game plan for dealing with unexpected issues or grievances that may arise.

➤ **FLEXIBILITY:** Expect that things might change over time or because of a single event, such as a major budget cut. As the serenity prayer suggests: Accept those things you cannot change. Be prepared to re-envision some of the moving parts of the partnership if necessary.

➤ **A NURTURED RELATIONSHIP:** Mutual respect is a starting place, but an ongoing partnership between organizations requires an investment of time and effort. Get to know the culture of your counterpart, establish opportunities for interaction, and celebrate partnership achievements (Effective Partnerships, 2014).

Although the partnerships bring many benefits, there are occasional pitfalls to consider. For example, when working with colleges and universities, you need to keep in mind that the academic calendar at a university will differ from the K–12 school calendar. College mentors may be unavailable during winter and spring breaks. Similarly, college students may require a flexible schedule during finals and midterms to accommodate their testing schedule. With adequate communication and flexibility these challenges can be overcome.

Another aspect to consider is that although the college mentors have technical expertise, they may lack teaching experience. These students are not necessarily certified teachers. At A.D. Sullivan School, the college mentors teach alongside certified teachers during the after-school program. This model has worked particularly well. We have found that the combination of content and curriculum, or pedagogy, specialists is a complementary one.

PARENTS AS PARTNERS

Parents can serve as valuable partners in building a STEM Lab. Access to expertise is one reason to involve parents. As Rabbi Gary Menchel notes: "We have a number of parents who are very involved in technology. We call on their ideas and expertise because they are out there working in the real world. Our program benefits from their expertise" (interview, May 13, 2018). A quick parent survey using Google Forms is one way to find parents with professional STEM qualifications. Parents can be invited to serve as guest speakers on a STEM Career Day and can help find potential venues for STEM internships for high school students. One parent at the A.D. Sullivan School, who is a medical doctor, purchased DNA kits for second-grade students and then co-taught a hands-on lesson on extracting DNA from a strawberry. In many cases, the Parent Teacher Organization helps to grow and sustain the STEM Lab with fundraising.

Parent involvement in STEM and support for the STEM Lab, however, is not a given. Many parents are unfamiliar with the acronym, may have limited background or experience in STEM, or may feel uncomfortable helping their children with STEM homework or projects. Overall, parent engagement needs to be cultivated. The goals of STEM "professional development" for parents are to: develop awareness of the importance of STEM in their child's education and future; increase their understanding of and comfort level with STEM through hands-on experiences; and feel encouraged to support STEM learning outside of school hours.

The A.D. Sullivan School adopted the Latinas in STEM approach to parent education, which promotes parent involvement in special STEM events, such as the STEM 101 Conference. At the conference, students participate in a variety of hands-on STEM activities, while their parents attend workshops. As a bilingual magnet school, A.D. Sullivan serves a population that is 30 percent Spanish speaking; therefore parent workshops are offered in both English and Spanish. First, parents are invited to attend an introduction to STEM workshop. Next, financial literacy workshops encourage parents to begin planning for their child's college education. Coupled with this workshop, parents learn about STEM careers and pathways for pursuing STEM education in a small career fair featuring representatives from STEM organizations and local colleges. The STEM 101 Conference ends with a collaborative engineering challenge, in which parents and children apply design thinking and experience the excitement of project-based learning.

The STEM 101 Conference is not the only opportunity for parent participation and learning. Over the course of the year, parents are invited to accompany their children to off-campus activities at local colleges, the science museum, or other places that host STEM events. Overall, the goal is to increase the parents' knowledge and awareness, so that they will seek out extracurricular activities for their children, such as a STEM summer camp, community-based activities on weekends, and projects that can be done at home.

STEM 101 Conferences, field trips, STEM career fair, engineering challenges—what do these have to do with the STEM Lab? If you have begun to suspect that the STEM Lab is one tool, albeit an important one, for creating a strong STEM culture in the school, then you have discovered the big idea within this effort. The STEM Lab is a location for STEM learning, but not the only one in a school. It should be an engine for change encouraging STEM exploration throughout the school, an environment that encourages interdisciplinary, project-based learning, and an exemplar of digital age education at its best.

Another approach for involving parents is to invite them to visit their child's classroom for a few hours on a specific day of the month. Celebrating Parent's Day on a monthly basis is a wonderful way to maintain a positive rapport with parents. If designed properly, it's also a means of engaging the parents with the content. This is a good way to promote interest in STEM, if during these visits parents are invited to the STEM Lab to engage in hands-on exploration with their children.

STEM LAB STORY
STEM/STEAM GEORGIA, ATLANTA, GEORGIA

STEM/STEAM Georgia is an arm of the Department of Education (DOE) with responsibility for developing effective STEM education in Georgia's schools. One of the goals of the Georgia DOE is to encourage schools to develop a strong STEM culture to support learning. The Georgia DOE encourages K–12 schools to apply for the state-sponsored STEM or STEAM certification. Currently, about 70 Georgia schools have STEM certification and seven have the more recently available STEAM certification.

The applications for STEM/STEAM certification (stemgeorgia.org) outline the essential elements of a strong STEM program. Certification is offered for elementary, middle school, and high school levels. Each application is a ten-page questionnaire that asks for documentation of a school's STEM/STEAM vision and culture, relevant modes of instruction, content knowledge and professional development, STEM/STEAM integration into the overall curriculum, the presence of STEM/STEAM Labs, and active community, business, or higher education partnerships. As Meghan McFerrin, the Georgia STEM/STEAM Program Specialist, explains:

> *We want our schools to develop what STEM or STEAM really means for them and for the students at their school in their community, and how that connects to local business and community partnerships. That is the big piece. It's all about the application of (STEM/STEAM) and preparing students for careers (interview, June 11, 2018).*

STEM/STEAM Georgia provides each participating school with guidelines for the required partnerships and specific definitions for a partner's involvement in the school. Involvement is measured at three levels: support, interactive, and advocate (Principles of Effective Partnerships, n.a., p.1). The level of participation is determined by the type and frequency of participation by the partner. "No two schools are alike and no two partnerships are alike. It depends upon the school and the capacity of the partner," offers Felicia Cullen, the DOE's other STEM/STEAM Program Specialist (interview, June 11, 2018).

A partner may:

➤ Contribute expertise, content, or materials to the school's STEM/STEAM curriculum and instruction, which is structured as project-based learning;

➤ Serve as a host for "student field trips, job shadowing, or internships";

➤ Mentor students in the process of designing solutions for real world problems;

➤ Sponsor STEM/STEAM competitions;

➤ Provide PD for teachers; and

➤ Make donations of funds or hardware.

(Georgia DOE, n.a., para. 1)

It is interesting to note that STEM/STEAM certification also requires evidence that the partnership is promoting a STEM/STEAM culture in the school. This references the quality of the relationship, describing an active and visible role for the partner in the day-to-day life of the school.

Here are a few examples of STEM/STEAM partnerships in Georgia schools:

➤ Approximately one-third of Georgia's students attend rural schools (Sampson, 2016). A recently certified school in the Blue Ridge Mountain district of northern Georgia has a partnership with a local apple orchard. The orchard business has moved some of its research to the school, where students help them to determine the best time of year to grow different varieties of apple.

➤ Warner Robins, Georgia, which lies about 90 miles southeast of Atlanta, is home to the Museum of Aviation, a United States Air Force aerospace museum. The Museum of Aviation partners with local middle schools on a variety of aerospace engineering projects. One recent museum-based event that included a rocket-building competition, was sponsored by the Society of American Military Engineers (SAME). SAME President Colonel Jim Hickman describes the goal of this program: "By partnering with local schools, we can reach out to youth and enhance their knowledge in (STEM) fields . . . and hopefully inspire them to pursue careers in those fields and potentially cultivate talented, engaged future Reserve Citizen Airmen" (Ebarb, 2017, para. 3).

➤ The addition of STEAM certification was in large measure due to the tremendous growth of the film business in Georgia (private conversation, June 11, 2018). Georgia now ranks as the third largest film production location in the U.S., after New York and Los Angeles (Dominey, 2018). The Georgia Film Academy (GFA), established by the University System of Georgia and Technical College System of Georgia in 2015, provides training for the thousands of jobs that support film production. Toward this goal of creating a pipeline of workers for the industry, GFA also actively partners with schools in a statewide program that provides PD for film teachers and a film production curriculum for high schools (Brett, 2017).

➤ Many schools in rural Georgia that do not have access to partnerships with industry must use available local resources, which are typically related to agriculture. These schools get support from small businesses, civic organizations, and local farmers. According to STEM/STEAM Georgia, the focus on agriscience also highlights an important career pathway. McFerrin acknowledges: "Agriscience is a huge industry. Many of our students have a negative perception of what agriculture is and aren't aware that they can make a good living by working in agriscience. Schools in Ware County have been able to tap into the large agriculture department at Fort Valley State University and embed agriculture instruction in their STEM programs" (interview, June 11, 2018).

Regarding parents as partners, the STEM/STEAM certification process includes feedback from parents. The DOE is interested to know how STEM/STEAM learning affects home life. Cullen relates: "We hear about the positive impact from the parents of students from many different backgrounds. They say things such as: 'My child comes home and now things that we would have thrown out otherwise become building tools.' 'The kids are always asking questions about why and how.' The big change they observe is from kids sitting in front of the TV to wanting to teach their parents how to garden. STEM/STEAM education has had a very powerful impact" (interview, June 11, 2018).

CHAPTER 4 RECAP

Community partnerships are a valuable tool for building a successful STEM Lab. A few of the key points regarding partnerships as opportunities are:

➤ Strategic partnerships can support your vision, increase capacity, and build sustainability.

➤ Seek and you will find. There are endless possibilities for establishing partnerships within and outside of your community beginning with local businesses, industry, and local colleges and universities. It all begins with networking.

➤ Look for the win-win. Partnerships are about a mutual benefit.

➤ The benefits of partnerships can come in the form of grants, professional development, programs, materials, and resources.

From an in-depth discussion of external partnerships in this chapter, the focus of Chapter 5 will be your most important partners within the school: the teachers. Without a doubt, ongoing support and training for teachers fuels the STEM Lab engine.

5

PD THAT FITS TO A T (AS IN TECHNOLOGY)

Why do we have a STEM Lab? A huge amount of the credit goes to our STEM director. She's been attending ISTE for close to 20 years. Each year she comes back and shares what she learned.

**—RABBI JONATHAN KNAPP,
PRINCIPAL, YAVNEH ACADEMY, PARAMUS, NEW JERSEY**

DRIVING QUESTIONS

➤ Why are teachers the key to building a STEM Lab?

➤ What kind of professional development (PD) is needed to support learning in a STEM Lab?

➤ How can ISTE Standards for Educators and Students support PD?

➤ Are there PD options for every budget?

THE TEACHER'S ROLE

A STEM Lab has the potential to encourage overall, transformational change in a school. This type of change has goals, but it does not really have an end point. It is a continuous improvement process of researching, planning, training, implementing, evaluating, and then beginning the cycle again from the next point of experience and understanding. As we discussed earlier, school leaders have an important role in creating a vision and bringing others on board. It is the teachers, however, who are on the front lines of transformational change.

One of the challenges of innovation in a school setting is that teachers are not entirely of the same mind regarding the necessary changes. Snyder (2017) suggests that there are four teacher perspectives regarding change:

➤ **THE EARLY ADOPTER** is the one that enthusiastically embraces the professional learning and teaching challenges involved in change.

➤ **THE CLASSROOM COMPLIANT** accept change, but conserve their energy while focusing upon the students who cross their threshold every day" (Snyder 2017, p. 4).

➤ **THE DISILLUSIONED SKEPTIC** is a committed and dedicated teacher who feels she has simply seen the school jump on one too many of the latest trends only to see them fail.

➤ **THE ACTIVE OPPOSITION** are vocal, will try to "thwart any improvements that may threaten them, and use their political power to keep their life easy" (p. 4).

Snyder (2017) also observed that these viewpoints are not found in exclusively veteran or novice teachers. Veteran teachers, among them Baby Boomers, can be as enthusiastic about learning and integrating new technologies as their digital native counterparts.

There are a few issues that trigger resistance in teachers. The first is a concern that the change will influence their relationship with the students (Goodson, Moore, & Hargreaves, 2006). Teachers are stressed by the increasing demand for technology integration, escalating curricular expectations, and accountability for student test scores. The focus is less on the teacher-student bond and more on technology-facilitated student learning. Especially when the teacher is also learning new technologies along with the students, the relationship may feel off-balance.

The second issue is that teachers fear loss of autonomy (Snyder, 2017). In a traditional classroom, the door is closed and the teacher is in charge of how and when the curriculum is covered. Interdisciplinary learning requires collaboration and sharing prep periods with other teachers. Project-based learning requires more imagination and elbow grease than lectures and worksheets. Further, when the work is done in a public and transparent environment such as a STEM Lab, the teacher may feel a loss of power because his/her planning and teaching skills are exposed.

Finally, Snyder (2017) cautions school leaders not to assume that resistance is always about avoiding extra work. Some resistant teachers may be sincerely concerned that the change will have a negative impact on the students. Research suggests that engaging the teachers in "clarifying conversations" about the planned change is a valuable investment of time (Snyder, 2017, p. 10). An example of a clarifying question is: "I can tell that you are concerned about taking time from your usual lessons to work on project-based learning in the STEM Lab. Can you tell me more about your specific concerns so that we can work out a solution?" Clarifying conversations strengthen the teachers' sense of ownership and increase their commitment to change because they have an authentic share in its leadership (Fullan, 2016; Leithwood & Seashore Lewis, 2012). This kind of dialogue prepares the foundation for professional development, which is a critical component of the change process.

ISTE STANDARD
EMPOWERING LEADER

Leaders create a culture where teachers and learners are empowered to use technology in innovative ways to enrich teaching and learning. Education leaders:

2a. Empower educators to exercise professional agency, build teacher leadership skills and pursue personalized professional learning.

Leaders can leverage the STEM Lab as a vehicle for transformational change within a school. This transformation begins with amplifying "teacher voice" and providing choice in professional learning.

UNPACKING TPACK

We describe best practices in STEM education as interdisciplinary, project-based, technology-facilitated learning that promotes inquiry, employs design thinking, and fosters a growth mindset. Professional development that supports continuous improvement for educators in any one of the above areas is a challenge. Taken together, the subject matter and methodology requirements of STEM education present even more of a challenge. The Technological Pedagogical Content Knowledge (TPACK) Framework is a helpful graphic organizer that can be used to illustrate the relationships between three types of knowledge: technology, content, and pedagogy, which intersect to form TPACK (Figure 5.1).

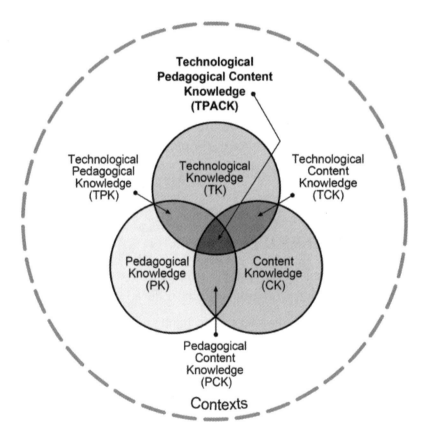

FIGURE 5.1 This is a graphic representation of the TPACK framework.
Source: tpack.org

TPACK serves to illustrate the "dynamic, transactional relationship between these components of knowledge" when they are applied in different contexts (Koehler, Shin, & Mishra, 2012, p. 16). Different dynamics are at play in different settings. The training and background of the teacher, the grade level targeted for the lessons, the culture and demographics of the students are among the factors that influence the outcomes of instruction. With this in mind, "every situation is unique, and no single combination of content, technology, and pedagogy will apply for every teacher, every course, or every view of teaching" (Koehler, 2012, para. 3). Effectively, TPACK is a reminder that content, pedagogy, and technological knowledge do not exist as silos. As you plan to prepare your faculty to work with complex STEM content in a STEM Lab environment, remember as well that there are many different issues and parameters that will influence the outcome.

ISTE STANDARDS AND YOUR PD TOOLKIT

Professional Development is also a means of encouraging a growth mindset for your faculty. The same digital age skills and emotional intelligences that we look to cultivate in our students must first be found in their role models and mentors: the teachers. The first step in PD is to not just to cultivate an understanding of STEM Education, but to foster the teacher's self-perception as someone capable of being an effective teacher in a new kind of learning environment. As Dirksen (2012) suggests, it is helpful to begin by asking the learners to think about what they already know about teaching STEM, what they hypothesize about teaching STEM, and what learning gaps they think might be present. This process reinforces the feelings of agency and self-actualization in the learner.

The ISTE Standards for Educators are a tool for framing discussions around STEM professional development. These standards encourage teachers to deepen practice, collaborate with peers, and rethink traditional approaches to prepare students to drive their own learning (ISTE, 2017). Here is an overview of the Standards for Educators (specific indicators can be found at iste.org/standards/for-educators):

➤ **LEARNER:** Educators continually improve their practice by learning from and with others and exploring proven and promising practices that leverage technology to improve student learning.

   EXAMPLES: Attend PD workshops and conferences including ISTE, join professional learning communities, and participate in peer-to-peer coaching and collaboration.

➤ **LEADER:** Educators seek out opportunities for leadership to support student empowerment and success and to improve teaching and learning.

EXAMPLES: Encourage inquiry-based and project-based learning that is learner-centered; share examples of effective student empowerment in conference presentations and EdCamps; ask students to present their work at school or at an ISTE poster session.

➤ **CITIZEN:** Educators inspire students to positively contribute to and responsibly participate in the digital world.

EXAMPLES: Model responsible digital citizenship; engage students in reflective practice about their own digital activity.

➤ **COLLABORATOR:** Educators dedicate time to collaborate with both colleagues and students to improve practice, discover and share resources and ideas, and solve problems.

EXAMPLES: Set aside time, before or after school or during lunchtime for collaboration with a partner or small group; create a Google group, Padlet, or social bookmarking site for your collaborating team; join an ISTE online community, such as the Teacher Education Network or the STEM Network.

➤ **DESIGNER:** Educators design authentic, learner-driven activities and environments that recognize and accommodate learner variability.

EXAMPLES: If your school has a STEM Lab, then integrate lab work (project-based, inquiry-based, hands-on, design-thinking supported learning) into your curriculum. If your school does not yet have a STEM Lab, encourage school leaders to establish one and in the meanwhile, integrate lab work into your curriculum.

➤ **FACILITATOR:** Educators facilitate learning with technology to support student achievement of the ISTE Standards for Students.

EXAMPLES: Make sure that students have the skills and working equipment needed to access the technology; be prepared to address the concerns of students with all levels of ability and differing levels of interest.

➤ **ANALYST:** Educators understand and use data to drive their instruction and support students in achieving their learning goals.

EXAMPLES: Collect, analyze, and use data from a variety of sources, including electronic portfolios, standardized test results, and through the use of technology-based assessment tools, such as Flipgrid.

The standards can be used in a variety of ways for PD. For example, they can be used to create a professional growth rubric for your faculty; as a lens for analysis and critique of plans for the implementation of new initiatives in your school; or as a list of topics for faculty meeting discussions or full-length professional development sessions.

ISTE STANDARD
EMPOWERING LEADER

Leaders create a culture where teachers and learners are empowered to use technology in innovative ways to enrich teaching and learning. Education leaders:

2b. Build the confidence and competency of educators to put the ISTE Standards for Students and Educators into practice.

The STEM Lab is an ideal venue for students and educators to put ISTE Standards into practice. Lesson plans, electronic portfolios, and student self-reflections are examples of artifacts that can be used to identify the application of standards.

PD POSSIBILITIES FOR SCHOOLS OF ALL TYPES AND SIZES

When it comes to professional development, there is no such thing as one-size-fits-all. High school teachers are most often content specialists. Their PD needs may be directed toward equipment and safety certifications for the STEM Lab. Elementary school teachers are often generalists and may need more guidance in the substance of interdisciplinary learning for STEM subjects, as well as in the types of technologies that are typically found in a STEM Lab. Middle school teachers may find themselves in a position between the two, with stronger skills in one or another STEM content area and needing support in navigating interdisciplinary learning and teaching the foundations of design thinking through project-based learning.

In addition, public schools and private schools have different PD frameworks. Private schools may be less constrained regarding content, but more constrained regarding budget. Public schools have the benefit of collaborative professional learning days that are set aside for teacher professional development, but may be limited by district determined initiatives. In the last analysis, school leaders need to be creative with whatever time and resources are available.

Some of the key questions regarding PD are: Who is to receive the training? How will it be delivered? When and where will it take place? Who will provide it? How often? How much will it cost? The answers to these questions are likely to vary from school to school.

TOP TEN CONTENDERS FOR STEM LAB PD

To help you find a good match for your STEM Lab PD, here is a list of the top ideas suggested by the contributors to this book, in no particular order.

1. **COMMON PLANNING TIME:** This is a designated period when teachers in different subject areas or grade level classrooms come together to design projects that promote interdisciplinary learning. In some school districts, five prep periods are mandated by union contract. One option is to create a sixth common planning period specifically for the purpose of STEM integration and PD in project-based learning at your school (Martha Osei-Yaw).

2. **TECH IN TWENTY:** This is an example of in-house PD provided by members of the STEM Lab team in sessions lasting 20 minutes. It is a way to introduce teachers to new technology tools or reinforce learning over lunch. It also allows the team to build a relationship with teachers and to learn which teachers might need one-on-one follow-up. Another "taste of technology" method is to use five minutes of grade level or faculty meetings before or after school to introduce a tool from the lab (Chani Lichtiger, Yavneh Academy).

3. **COMMUNITY MAKERSPACES:** Workshops and multi-session courses on CAD software, 3D printing, Arduino, hydroponics, drones, and other topics and tools of the STEM Lab are frequent offerings at community makerspaces. Some makerspaces specifically target teachers by providing training during summer vacation (Deborah Nagler).

4. **EDCAMPS:** An EdCamp is a free "unconference" organized by and for teachers. At the beginning of an EdCamp, the participants determine which sessions will be presented. It is an opportunity for passionate STEM teachers and STEM Lab leaders to recruit interest and feedback on their work (Marcos Navas, Rolando Monserrat).

5. **PEER-TO-PEER COACHING:** The enthusiastic early adopters in your faculty can also be helpful and influential resources for PD. Teachers, whose participation in professional conferences or other types of training is sponsored by the school, can be drafted to pay their experience forward in training sessions for the rest of the faculty. This is not only a multiplier for your PD dollars; learning from a colleague can also generate increased interest and motivation among peers (Martha Osei-Yaw). In addition, support staff such as reading specialists, math coaches, media specialists, and tech coaches can be instrumental in providing professional development and building capacity at the school level (Marcos Navas).

6. **UNIVERSITY-SOURCED PD:** Often institutions for higher education offer professional development programs for local schools. Look for offerings in STEM subject matter, Next Generation Science Standards, and instructional practice (Kirk Brown). Student organizations within higher education institutions are another source for training (Martha Osei-Yaw).

7. **PROFESSIONAL CONFERENCES AND PROGRAMS:** ISTE is one of the many exceptional multi-day conferences that are available both nationally and locally. For example, the Buck Institute for Education (BIE.org) and the High Tech High Graduate School of Education (hthgse.edu/professional-education/institutes) offer professional development in project-based learning. Constructing Modern Knowledge (constructingmodernknowledge.com) is a four-day innovation and project-based learning experience for teachers (Steve Freedman, Tikvah Wiener).

8. **TWITTER PD:** Twitter is a versatile and free tool for ongoing PD. It can be used for research on STEM or project-based learning topics. The school leader or STEM Lab team can tweet links to articles and resources to the faculty. The teachers can be invited to curate a Twitter Chat on a topic relevant to STEM (Martha Osei-Yaw).

9. **STEM LAB MENTORS:** Particularly in elementary school settings, where teachers are generalists, the faculty may have different levels of familiarity with the technology in the STEM Lab. A very practical approach, allowing that the STEM Lab educators are not inundated with requests, is for the team to provide one-on-one mentoring on an as-needed basis (Stephanie Talalai, Chani Lichtiger). Another kind of mentor that can be useful, particularly in high schools, is industry professionals who are willing to mentor and advise faculty regarding real-world projects and best practices in their field (Dave Janosz).

10. **DISTRICT-SPONSORED PD:** Reach out to the central office of your school district to find out if they can provide professional development. There may be subject area supervisors or master teachers available to lead training upon request (Martha Osei-Yaw).

* **SAFETY TRAINING:** Technically this would be an eleventh offering on the list, but we are putting a special emphasis on this type of training because it is a must for every STEM Lab that houses electrical, electronic, or power tools. All faculty members who will be using the lab, including the experts in high school labs, should be certified in the safe use of machinery. Safety training should be reviewed and updated continually as the STEM Lab acquires new equipment (Dave Janosz).

The above list is certainly not comprehensive. As schools with growing STEM education programs, including STEM Labs, address the challenges of providing PD for their teachers, additional, creative approaches will emerge. Ongoing professional development for school leaders and technology coaches is a way to keep abreast of PD options and developments in the field.

ISTE STANDARD
EMPOWERING LEADER

Leaders create a culture where teachers and learners are empowered to use technology in innovative ways to enrich teaching and learning. Education leaders:

3c. Inspire a culture of innovation and collaboration that allows the time and space to explore and experiment with digital tools.

3d. Support educators in using technology to advance learning that meets the diverse learning, cultural, and social-emotional needs of individual students.

GREAT PD IDEAS FROM A.D SULLIVAN

A.D. Sullivan School is an example of a PK–5 school that began a STEM Lab on a shoestring budget. How did they manage to provide serious PD for their faculty at that crucial stage? Necessity is the mother of invention, and Martha is the master of finding and optimizing opportunities. She used multiple sources to put together consistent and impactful PD to support the school's newly founded STEM Lab. Here are a few examples:

1. **DISTRICT-FUNDED PD:** Martha jumped at the opportunity to sign her school up for a district-funded, after-school program in Tinkercad and 3D printing for fourth-grade students. Only three schools were chosen in the first year of the program and Martha's school was one of the first to enroll. The program also included training in Tinkercad and 3D printing for a cadre of teachers from the school. The training had two parts. First the teachers went to the offices of PicoTurbine to learn how to operate the equipment and the software. The second phase of the training was conducted by a PicoTurbine staff member during the after-school program. The teachers trained side by side with the students.

2. **SCHOOL BUDGET-FUNDED PD:** The Hybrid Program conducted at Liberty Science Center was another source for STEM Lab–related PD for the school. The program consisted of a weekly student and teacher STEM laboratory workshop that took place over a six-week period. The lessons were aligned with the New Jersey Student Learning Standards and the Next Generation Science Standards. The program gave the students an opportunity to work through the design thinking process as they completed an engineering design challenge. The teacher component of the program consisted of hands-on training on utilizing Tinkercad and the use of 3D printers. The teachers involved in the Hybrid program were not the same teachers as those involved in the after-school program, Project Enable.

3. **SHARED LEADERSHIP:** One of the first things that Martha did when the school leaders decided to build the STEM Lab was to enroll the Math Specialist as a faculty leader for the program. The responsibilities of this role included organizing and supporting peer-to-peer coaching. Although the Math Specialist was not the director of the STEM Lab in an official capacity, she frequently made herself available to help teachers who were using the lab.

4. **PEER-TO-PEER (FREE PD):** What school leaders learned in the process of both of the above programs was that the teachers in both cohorts were able to use their newly acquired skills set to support one another throughout the year. The peer-to-peer coaching and support was an organic process, which provided the foundation for other teacher-to-teacher training initiatives within the school.

5. **PROFESSIONAL LEARNING COMMUNITY (PLC):** A PLC is a group of people who are interested in developing their skills and knowledge in an area of education. In A.D. Sullivan School, leaders established a weekly common planning time to be used for Professional Learning Communities. School leaders can encourage the support staff to facilitate PD that can enhance the STEM Curriculum. At one of the schools, the support staff facilitated PD on project-based lessons with a STEM focus. This professional development was free of cost to the school and the training was provided during the course of the day (Figure 5.2).

FIGURE 5.2 PD in action: Teachers at A.D. Sullivan learn robotics.
Source: M. Osei-Yaw

6. **GRANT-FUNDED PD:** By partnering with the Liberty Science Center, A.D. Sullivan School was able to obtain a grant from the Clare Foundation. This grant funded a program that provided free STEM workshops for three kindergarten classes from the school, as well as PD for the teachers. All of the programming was free of cost and was provided onsite by Liberty Science Center staff. The program also included a free family night at the Science Center for the students, parents, and teachers.

7. **HIGHER EDUCATION STUDENT ORGANIZATION:** After a group of students at A.D. Sullivan formed a junior chapter of the Society of Hispanic Professional Engineers (SHPE), members of the NJIT SHPE chapter came to the school and provided workshops for junior chapter members and their advisors. The projects presented dealt with civil engineering, chemical engineering, computer engineering, and so forth. The teacher advisors for the chapter were inspired to replicate the SHPE activities with the students in their classrooms and in other after-school programs.

How does one find PD opportunities on a shoestring budget? Here are our recommendations: Along with the parents, students, and faculty, invite local politicians, district leadership, faculty members and students from a nearby university, and other schools to participate in your school's STEM events. Read and respond immediately to email communications (district and other) about STEM offerings. Network everywhere to build connections with new resources. Most importantly, don't be afraid to fly your STEM flag! Take every opportunity to communicate your vision and passion for STEM education and your belief that a STEM Lab is important. When people know that you are interested, they will be more likely to share information about STEM opportunities.

STEM LAB STORY
YAVNEH ACADEMY, PARAMUS, NEW JERSEY

Although the combination STEM Lab/Makerspace at Yavneh Academy opened a year ago, Principal Rabbi Jonathan Knapp says that building the lab has taken something close to a decade. This school primarily uses ISTE conferences for STEM professional development. Rabbi Knapp explained the role that ISTE has played in the process of transforming the school:

> If you take a look back at our financial investment in PD over the past decade, you would see an almost unusually high proportion went towards sending teachers to ISTE. We send 10 to 12 people each year: a combination of faculty, administration, and the STEM staff. I, myself, have attended twice. I think that speaks to our commitment.
>
> We're getting great value from the ISTE immersive environment—the energy, diversity of the attendees, and types of experiences that are happening there. We see an impact on the school. It's been about 12 years and if you sprinkle ISTE training in enough grade levels, you see the results. It starts with one or two integrated units and starts to spread throughout the school. (interview, May 23, 2018)

Rabbi Knapp describes the ISTE experience as one that is taken very seriously by his staff and teacher: "We push really hard and it is exhausting. At the end of each day's sessions, the cohort gathers for a few hours to unpack and really plumb the depths of what they've learned." A week or two after the conference, the group reconvenes at the school to continue the discussion of what parts of ISTE learning can be brought into their classrooms. Attending ISTE is a commitment. Participants are expected to bring back technology integrated, innovative lessons for their students, as well as ideas and inspiration to share with their colleagues. He concludes: "ISTE has given us a great return on the investment."

The Board of Education also plays an active role in the school. It is a governing body with regard to the curriculum and programs of the school, but Rabbi Knapp describes it as something more like a think tank. It is comprised of "educators, parents in the school community that have a background in education, psychology, and sometimes medicine." Educating the Board of Education was an important part of the process of building the STEM Lab. They "read articles and books together, attended workshops, visited other schools locally and in New York City." In his view, these activities were "a huge impetus" for moving forward with the decision to build a STEM Lab.

Professional development for his faculty and his Board of Education are part of Rabbi Knapp's commitment to continuous improvement. He says: "We just opened the STEM Lab and we still feel the need to upgrade and improve it. It is a process; it's never done." His advice to schools that are just beginning to build a STEM Lab: "Don't be afraid to start small. Every time you do something, you will know that there are 99 other things you weren't able to do yet. Don't get discouraged." A STEM Lab is a marathon, not a sprint.

CHAPTER 5 RECAP

Teachers are the driving force behind successful implementation of a STEM Lab. Engaging and training the faculty is the first priority and challenge:

➤ A STEM Lab has the potential to encourage overall, transformational change in a school beginning with the role of the teacher.

➤ Professional development is a continuous improvement process of researching, planning, training, implementing, and evaluating.

➤ The ISTE Standards for Educators can be used to create a professional growth rubric for your faculty; as a lens for analysis and critique of plans for the implementation of new initiatives in your school; or as a list of topics for faculty meeting discussions or full-length professional development sessions.

➤ PD funding and opportunities can come from a variety of different sources, including your school or district, peer coaching among your teachers, professional learning communities, grand-funded programs, and university-sponsored programs.

From an overview of the challenges and opportunities associated with professional development, we focus next on how the curriculum aligns with learning in a STEM Lab. Standards, interdisciplinary learning, and the selection of effective lessons for the STEM Lab are the focus of Chapter 6.

6 AT THE INTERSECTION OF STEM LAB AND CURRICULUM

I can envision a cohesive K–12 STEM program, where departments are integrated. It is very difficult to teach students who come to high school with no foundation in STEM. We need to capture excitement that the students have in early elementary grades and build upon it year after year.

**—ROLANDO MONSERRAT,
DIRECTOR STEM ACADEMY, TEANECK HIGH SCHOOL**

DRIVING QUESTIONS

➤ What does it mean to implement an interdisciplinary, standards-based approach?

➤ What is the intersection of school curriculum and STEM Lab?

➤ Where can you find curricular materials for schools at different levels?

STANDARDS, INTERDISCIPLINARY CURRICULUM, AND THE STEM LAB

The purpose of the STEM Lab is to provide a framework for project-based learning, which provides "authentic learning experiences connected to real-world problems, tools, and materials" (Wardrip & Brahms, 2016, p. 98). Through hands-on activity, learners explore multiple pathways for addressing the learning objectives of the curriculum. Alignment with the curriculum is the common denominator between school-based STEM/STEAM Labs, makerspaces, Fab Labs, and so forth.

As a rule, public school curricula are prepared on the district level. These curricula offer a framework for the content that needs to be delivered in the classroom, along with suggested activities, and resources. All curricula developed on a district level are aligned to state and national standards.

Standards are defined as instructional goals or benchmarks for student achievement. ISTE Standards for Students, the Next Generation Science Standards (NGSS), and National Council of Teachers of Mathematics (NCTM) Principles and Standards are examples of national standards that offer a compass for STEM curriculum and instruction.

ISTE STANDARDS FOR STUDENTS

Here is an overview of the ISTE Standards for Students (specific indicators can be found at www.iste.org/standards/for-students):

1. **EMPOWERED LEARNER:** Students leverage technology to take an active role in choosing, achieving, and demonstrating competency in their learning goals, informed by the learning sciences.

2. **DIGITAL CITIZEN:** Students recognize the rights, responsibilities, and opportunities of living, learning, and working in an interconnected digital world, and they act and model in ways that are safe, legal, and ethical.

3. **KNOWLEDGE CONSTRUCTOR:** Students critically curate a variety of resources using digital tools to construct knowledge, produce creative artifacts, and make meaningful learning experiences for themselves and others.

4. **INNOVATIVE DESIGNER:** Students use a variety of technologies within a design process to identify and solve problems by creating new, useful, or imaginative solutions.

5. **COMPUTATIONAL THINKER:** Students develop and employ strategies for understanding and solving problems in ways that leverage the power of technological methods to develop and test solutions.

6. **CREATIVE COMMUNICATOR:** Students communicate clearly and express themselves creatively for a variety of purposes using the platforms, tools, styles, formats, and digital media appropriate to their goals.

7. **GLOBAL COLLABORATOR:** Students use digital tools to broaden their perspectives and enrich their learning by collaborating with others and working effectively in teams locally and globally.

NGSS STANDARDS

The NGSS are built on the National Research Council's Framework of Three Dimensions (3D): "practices," "crosscutting ideas," and "disciplinary core ideas" (NGSS, 2018, para. 1). Practices focus on inquiry-based learning that employs design thinking. Crosscutting concepts are ideas that can be found and applied in every field of science. These include: "Patterns, similarity, and diversity; Cause and effect; Scale, proportion and quantity; Systems and system models; Energy and matter; Structure and function; Stability and change" (NGSS, 2018, para.4). An example of a crosscutting idea in the NGSS engineering standards is:

> **THE INFLUENCE OF SCIENCE, ENGINEERING, AND TECHNOLOGY ON SOCIETY AND THE NATURAL WORLD:** *All human activity draws on natural resources and has both short- and long-term consequences, positive as well as negative, for the health of people and the natural environment. (MS-ETS1-1)*
>
> *The uses of technologies and any limitations on their use are driven by individual or societal needs, desires, and values; by the findings of scientific research; and by differences in such factors as climate, natural resources, and economic conditions. (MS-ETS1-1) (NGSS, 2013).*

Disciplinary core ideas are concepts that are recognized in various scientific fields. They assist the learner in solving complex problems and connect the learning to real-world experiences and concerns. An example of one of the disciplinary core ideas for engineering is:

> **DEFINING AND DELIMITING ENGINEERING PROBLEMS:** *The more precisely a design task's criteria and constraints can be defined, the more likely it is that the designed solution will be successful. Specification of constraints includes consideration of scientific principles and other relevant knowledge that are likely to limit possible solutions. (MS-ETS1-1)*

> *Disciplinary core ideas are suitable for multiple grade levels and can be presented in "increasing levels of depth and sophistication" (NGSS Lead States, 2013, para. 5).*

NCTM STANDARDS

The NCTM offers five content and five process standards. The content standards, as one might expect, reflect Mathematics topics that include: "Number & operations, Algebra, Geometry, Measurement, and Data analysis & probability" (NCTM, 2018, para. 4). The five process standards are "problem solving, reasoning & proof, communication, connections, and representation" (NCTM, 2018, para. 5). These process standards tie into project-based learning in the STEM Lab in numerous ways. For example, the representation standard states that students will be able to "use representations to model and interpret physical, social, and mathematical phenomena" (Problem solving, 2018, para. 5). Creating models is an integral part of the design process and one that is supported by the application of mathematics.

In fact, the essence of STEM is the understanding that these four disciplines, namely science, technology, engineering, and mathematics, share common and complementary principles and tools. The standards-based, interdisciplinary learning that defines STEM education defines the STEM Lab as well. For example, a popular STEM Lab project is a unit on building a bridge (College of Engineering, University of Colorado, 2017). Science is represented in the study of weather-related and geology-related bridge-design considerations. Technology is represented in weather-forecasting tools,

3D design applications, and search engines used to gather information. Engineering frames the exploration of bridge types, tension and compression forces, as well as design considerations such as "loads, piers/columns and girders/beams" and "strength of materials." Mathematics is present in all of the discussion of building economics, including estimates and costs.

Among the standards that this unit addresses are:

- ➤ **NGSS SCIENCE STANDARD:** Evaluate competing design solutions using a systematic process to determine how well they meet the criteria and constraints of the problem.

- ➤ **ISTE STANDARDS FOR STUDENTS:** Innovative Designer—Students use a variety of technologies within a design process to identify and solve problems by creating new, useful, or imaginative solutions.

- ➤ **NGSS ENGINEERING STANDARDS:** Develop a model to generate data for iterative testing and modification of a proposed object, tool, or process such that an optimal design can be achieved.

- ➤ **NCTM MATHEMATICS STANDARDS:** Create and use representations to organize, record, and communicate mathematical ideas:

  - ➤ Select, apply, and translate among mathematical representations to solve problems;

  - ➤ Use representations to model and interpret physical, social, and mathematical phenomena.

BRINGING STEM LAB ACTIVITY INTO THE CURRICULUM

The dynamics of the integration of STEM Lab activity into the curriculum will differ from school to school, whether public or private. "A major hurdle in implementing project-based curricula is that they require simultaneous changes in curriculum, instruction, and assessment—changes that are often foreign to the students as well as the teachers" (Barron, et al., 1998). Standards, as described above, can help with the transition from traditionally siloed instruction to an interdisciplinary approach. Professional development and professional learning communities can be used to train and support teachers. Student voice and choice, as will be discussed in Chapter 8, can be cultivated. Still there are other issues that may arise and will require flexibility and creativity.

One potential roadblock in introducing project-based learning into the curriculum is pacing. Some public school districts require strict adherence to a district-wide calendar for instruction, while others are more flexible. If you work in a district or school where curriculum development is autonomous, then state and national standards, as well as the examples of best practice by other schools, can be your guide for integrating the STEM Lab and the curriculum. The State of Maryland, for example, has a well-developed framework and curriculum for standards-based STEM instruction (See mdk12. msde.maryland.gov/instruction/curriculum/stem/index.html). If you work in a district or school with strict pacing requirements, then consider arranging opportunities for a media specialist or STEM curriculum to work with classroom teachers to help them work STEM Lab projects into the curriculum.

Of course there are schools that fall in the mid-range, where a standards-driven curriculum is available, but pacing is at the discretion of the teacher. In this case, the process of integrating use of the STEM Lab into the curriculum can be determined through the collaborative work of the school administration and faculty. The A.D. Sullivan school falls into this category of school regarding pacing. Theirs is one example of phased implementation of project-based learning in a STEM Lab.

Implementation of this initiative took place in several stages. In the first year of integration, the teachers of A.D. Sullivan School participated in training in project-based learning using the framework from the Buck Institute for Education. In the initial phase, a cadre of teachers was selected to take part in PD offered at the district level. These teachers then became peer coaches in project-based learning for the remainder of the faculty. They returned to the school and presented what they had learned to their grade-level partners. The peer coaches facilitated planning of a series of project-based learning lessons for every grade level. The school leaders were encouraged by the results of the peer-to-peer coaching, and they felt it was highly effective because the information was shared across the faculty in a way that was relevant and accessible. In addition, it provided a foundation for ongoing collaboration among the teachers.

Full implementation of this program began in year two. Each grade-level team developed a total of four projects during the course of the year—one for every marking period. Teachers implemented the projects during the Science block. All of the projects were aligned to the district's science curriculum and the NGSS and offered developmentally appropriate activities for each grade level.

ADDITIONAL STEM LAB CHALLENGES

"Oh no, not STEM . . . again!" One school leader shared this exact quote, which came from a teacher who was less than enthusiastic about the prospect of integrating the STEM Lab into her curriculum. Resistance to change is not surprising. It is only one of numerous hazards on the path to building a successful STEM Lab. If you are introducing project-based learning in a school where any of the following are true, you will likely face challenges:

➤ There is a deficit of visionary leadership.

➤ Content silos are entrenched.

➤ Standardized test scores drive instruction.

➤ There is a shortage of teachers for math and science.

➤ There are gaps in teachers' STEM content knowledge.

➤ Time and opportunities for PD are limited.

➤ Teacher buy-in is uneven.

If you encounter these obstacles, there is no simple antidote; these kinds of issues can challenge the whole system. We will, however, humbly venture to offer a few suggestions to consider.

ITEM ONE: LACK OF VISIONARY LEADERSHIP

Recruitment of stakeholders frequently takes time. Bottomless passion, a clear and easily communicated vision, and lots of data will help. Invite key leaders to see the STEM Lab in action, create videos that document your successes and showcase student enthusiasm, and generate press. STEM is a buzzword right now, but riding the wave requires effort and attention. Persist, and you will be likely to prevail!

ITEM TWO: CONTENT SILOS

Content silos have been the norm since before the first Industrial Revolution. In today's classrooms, interdisciplinary learning is still a relatively new paradigm for most teachers. We recommend that you enlist the help of the district curriculum department in developing a strategy for overcoming this challenge. Look at examples of best practice in other schools. Start with low-hanging fruit—the most easily achievable successes—to help generate motivation and momentum at the outset. Engage the early adopters on your faculty first.

ITEM THREE: STANDARDIZED TESTS

Lynch (2016) summarizes the shortcomings of standardized testing as teaching to the test: attempting to raise scores by focusing on borderline achievers, while ignoring low achievers; and the disproportionate emphasis on test scores as a measure of school achievement. Recognition of these issues has grown, and both internet and print media are filled with articles about a shift away from reliance on standardized testing. In the meantime, work around the test. The more you can engage your stakeholders in STEM Lab successes and share the excitement and work product of your students, the more you will be able to advance the cause of authentic, interdisciplinary, project-based learning. Make sure that STEM is news in your school.

ITEM FOUR: MATH AND SCIENCE TEACHERS MISSING IN ACTION

The lack of math and science teachers is a systemic problem that may be experienced to different degrees by different schools or districts. Keep in mind, today's STEM students will be the STEM teachers of tomorrow. As for now, the teacher supply chain needs to be addressed as a collaboration between state or district BOE and local teachers' colleges and universities. Individuals with professional training in STEM fields may be interested in fast-track programs that prepare them to teach in public schools.

ITEMS FIVE AND SIX: CONTENT KNOWLEDGE GAPS AND THE NEED FOR PD

Administrators, curriculum coordinators, and teachers need to work together to identify the gaps in content knowledge and identify resources for filling them. The walls of the classroom are not boundaries. Information and expertise is available with the help of your media specialist, and content experts can visit the classroom via video chat. Local universities may be willing to recommend students who would like to serve as content specialists in STEM. Partnerships with colleges and universities can also be a source for professional development. Explore your community as well as outside networks for opportunities to build the knowledge and resources your classroom needs.

ITEM SEVEN: TEACHER RESISTANCE

Address—do not ignore—teachers' concerns about the project-based learning in the STEM Lab. Listen, be flexible, and offer training or targeted support if knowledge or skill gaps are the primary concern. Keep in mind there may be teachers who resist for other reasons. Be patient, as resistant players tend to come in line once the majority of the faculty is on board. In the meantime, draw upon your passion and vision to lead your colleagues toward the goal.

Even with a clearly defined goal, not everything will work the first time—but don't give up. You need to find what works for you. Resilience and persistence are part of the growth mindset; examine what worked and replicate it, find what didn't work and fine-tune that. Of course, this takes time and effort, but this is where commitment comes into play. Find colleagues who are invested in building a STEM Lab; connect with them to share successes and learn from failures. Attend ISTE, and you will see that you are not alone; in fact, the movement to support STEM learning is an international one.

FINDING THE RIGHT STEM LAB PROJECTS

Many volumes have been written on the subject of STEM curricula. There are at least 20 pages of STEM pedagogy and content books listed on Amazon, not to mention the burgeoning list of companies that are producing and distributing STEM curricula. With this in mind, here are a few suggested resources and helpful hints for navigating the bountiful sea of STEM teaching materials.

Although it is written with an eye toward the needs of the STEM teacher as a practitioner of project-based learning, we recommend *Invent to Learn: Making, Tinkering, and Engineering in the Classroom*, by Sylvia Libow Martinez and Gary Stager. This is an excellent book for school leaders and tech coaches who wish to understand what goes into a successful STEM Lab project. It provides a step-by-step analysis of how to plan the project, create effective prompts, and target the goal of an end product that is meaningful and enduring for the learner.

Aside from the many books on the market, the internet is a rich source for ideas. Teachers Pay Teachers is an online marketplace for teacher-designed lesson plans. LinkedIn, Pinterest, Twitter, and Instagram are also good resources. As always, the material needs to be vetted with an eye to your goals and the standards.

STEM LAB STORY
TEANECK HIGH SCHOOL, TEANECK, NEW JERSEY

A gleaming, three-foot trophy stands in a place of honor in Teaneck High School (THS). Next to the trophy, an engraved plaque lists the names of the two-dozen finalists in the New Jersey–based Panasonic Creative Design Challenge. The goal of this highly competitive robotics competition is to "engage and inspire young minds with a complex engineering and technology challenge" (Empowering a New Generation, 2018, para. 3). This year, the THS team is at the top of the list.

This win is a point of pride for THS, which was among the first high schools to recognize the importance of STEM education. In 2002, THS established the Technology Enriched Academy of Mathematics and Science (TEAMS). TEAMS is a four-year project-based learning program. TEAMS students spend the first two years in a cohort that studies computer science, science, mathematics, and technology-supported English language and the latter two in a course of study chosen by the student. TEAMS cohorts begin with roughly 40 ninth-grade students, but there is some attrition over the course of the program. TEAMS director, Rolando Monserrat attributes the attrition to the changing interests of the students. "It's random," suggests Monserrat." It crosses gender and ethnicity."

Beginning TEAMS students are introduced to the program with a survey course comprised of different STEM activities that center on the design process. As Monserrat told us, "these activities begin with a problem. The students need to study it and figure out what to do; then they build a prototype of the solution. Projects are developed through trial and error. Failure is a part of the solution. Without failure, you cannot move forward" (interview, May 10, 2018). Arduino, Lego Mindstorms robots, 3D printing, and aerospace simulations are a few of the subjects that are covered in the STEM course. The frustration for the teacher is that there is no STEM Lab in the school. All of the project-based learning takes place in and around a computer lab, where corners and closets are repurposed to house 3D printers, a laser cutter, electronics, robot parts, and tools (Figure 6.1). Monserrat describes the experience of teaching without a STEM Lab:

> Working on STEM projects without a STEM Lab is a little bit like trying to hit a homerun with my hands tied behind my back. We won the statewide competition, but it is difficult to compete on a national level because we do not yet have the space to work and to store large projects.

FIGURE 6.1 Students work in the classroom STEM Lab at Teaneck High School.
Source: Rolando Monserrat

He adds that the school did have typical workshop classrooms, including woodworking and machine shops at one time, but these spaces were converted for other purposes, such as a teacher prep area. Monserrat suggests that in the beginning of the digital era, computers were considered to be central. Only now has the focus shifted to hands-on work with a variety of new technologies. Still, this dynamic STEM teacher is committed to building a dedicated STEM Lab, and with passion and vision, he is likely to achieve this goal.

With more than a dozen years of work in standards-based, interdisciplinary learning at THS, Monserrat shares the following observations from the field:

First, quality equipment is critical. When he was rewriting the curriculum to include 3D printing about four years ago, Monserrat researched and eventually purchased some of the best, most reliable models of 3D printers for the school. Buying more printers of lesser value that are liable to break down is not a good investment.

Second, common planning time for STEM teachers is key. When teachers from the mathematics, science, and computer science department meet, it is possible to coordinate activities and to support the work in each other's classes. It is also important to share the school's STEM capacity with the rest of the faculty. For example, Monserrat participates in a district-sponsored EdCamp, where he demonstrates how 3D printers can be used in different disciplines. He notes that, "in chemistry, you can create a model of molecular structure; in history you can find a library of printable artifacts on Thingiverse; and in astronomy, NASA has over 300 STL files that create models of the moon's surface, landing sites, and satellites."

Finally, and most importantly, Monserrat believes that a successful high school STEM program has its foundation in the fourth and fifth grades.

> *High school is too late. We need to hook the students on STEM when their real interest begins. By offering opportunities to learn coding, robotics, and by engaging them in real world projects in elementary and middle school, we are paving the way to STEM learning in high school, then college, and eventually STEM careers.*

Public schools, as stated earlier, typically have a STEM curriculum that has been set by the district. If you are following a district curriculum, look for the resources and projects that are recommended therein. If you are able to write your own curriculum, look at examples of best practice, such as the Maryland State Curriculum. States often collaborate with one another. So if your own state does not provide the resources that you need, ask if they can recommend another. For example, years ago, Deborah was researching a technology plan for a school in South Carolina and called the DOE for information about state standards. They provided information, but also kindly recommended that she contact the DOE in North Carolina, which was known for its outstanding work. Don't be afraid to network across county or state lines, as well as public and private school ones.

Here are a few key points to keep in mind when selecting curricula and STEM Lab projects:

➤ Always begin with your goals. Even if there is no cost to you, there is a price to be paid if you adopt STEM projects that don't meet your objectives.

➤ Compare notes with other schools at the same level and with similar objectives, to see if they have recommendations.

➤ Know the needs of your teachers—their skill and knowledge levels as well as their preferences. Both novice and veteran teachers may prefer turn-key lessons. An example of this kind of material is the Science Buddies kits. Involve teachers in the selection of the kits and encourage peer-to-peer coaching as their use spreads through the school.

➤ Be open and flexible, yet cautious about opportunities. As a school leader, you need to be aware of district and board policy. When in doubt, check it out.

➤ Be aware of district or institutional policies regarding grants. Vet the provider by doing research, visiting other schools to see the curriculum in action, and checking out portfolios or videos that illustrate success.

As an example of seizing the moment to acquire STEM curriculum resources, the A.D. Sullivan school comes to mind. Dr. Daniel Fried, a professor at Saint Peter's University, contacted Martha about bringing his research project, a curriculum called Biochemistry Literacy for Kids, to her school. Professor Fried claimed that he could teach college-level biochemistry concepts to third through fifth graders using models.

Martha listened, looked at the portfolio of his work with other schools, and viewed presentation about the program. She decided that the partnership offered a worthwhile opportunity for her students. Once she cleared the program with the district office, Dr. Fried was welcomed in the school. The biochemistry lessons turned out to be one of the highlights of the school year.

CHAPTER 6 RECAP

Project-based learning in a STEM Lab offers opportunities for authentic learning that engages students in real-world problem solving.

> ➤ STEM is by definition an interdisciplinary approach to learning, and today's schools use a standards-based approach to learning. Standards, such as those provided by NGSS, ISTE, and NCTM, provide the guidelines for student content learning and achievement at different grade levels.

> ➤ The STEM Lab is an important tool for the hands-on and inquiry-based learning that should be a part of every STEM curriculum.

> ➤ The educational marketplace, both in print and online, is filled with STEM projects and materials. When considering a curriculum or program: Always begin with your goals; network with other schools and school leaders; know the needs and abilities of your teachers; and be open, but cautious about freebies.

From insights regarding the place of a STEM Lab in a standards-based curriculum to suggestions for how to select and where to find STEM Lab ideas, Chapter 7 will paint a picture of options for STEM Lab administration.

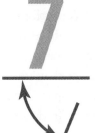

7
READY, SET . . . NOW IMPLEMENT

When I realized that certain technology needs were not being met by an external consultant, I taught myself networking and took over the network.

—ORLY NADLER,
MA'AYANOT YESHIVA HIGH SCHOOL FOR GIRLS, TEANECK, NEW JERSEY

DRIVING QUESTIONS

➤ What administrative challenges need to be addressed to insure smooth operation of your STEM Lab?

➤ What type of staff should there be in a STEM Lab? What are the staff's responsibilities?

➤ What is the best way to maintain student safety and security within the Lab?

ENSURING ALL THE PIECES ARE IN PLACE

If you build it, will they come? Not necessarily. Invariably, during the Q&A portion of our STEM Lab presentations, one or another disappointed STEM advocate will relate a failed attempt to launch a STEM Lab or the story of a STEM Lab that has closed. Sometimes it is due to the challenges mentioned in Chapter 6. Other reasons that we have heard are inadequate staffing, technical difficulties, competition for the space, and lack of time on the part of the teachers. Our goal is to set you up for success. To do so, let's recap some of the key concepts that we have discussed in the previous chapters.

First, putting all of the foundational pillars in place will help ensure a smooth launch for your STEM Lab. These include: developing a vision and recruiting stakeholders (supporters) for your vision; creating a plan with an appropriate budget; building partnerships; and integrating the STEM Lab and the curriculum. Clear expectations and laser-beam focus are required to make your dream STEM Lab a reality. To begin, you will need to identify the vision and goals for the lab. Ideally, the goals should have been developed by a core group of committed stakeholders, who will aid you in carrying out the vision. Once your goals are in place, you will need to figure out who will be responsible for overseeing the day-to-day operations of the STEM Lab. The "STEM Lab Administration 101" section of this chapter will address the issue of staffing in greater length.

Next, you will need to ensure that you have the equipment, materials, and resources you need to get started. A fully realized STEM Lab, including hardware, tools and equipment, a laptop cart and/or a bank of desktops, furniture, storage, materials, a SMART board, and a whiteboard, is a financial commitment. Schools with the benefit of a large budget may reach this target much more quickly than schools with limited funds. Everyone would rather be one of the former, but do not let funding deter you from getting started. It's better to start small and build as you go than to not start at all. One school started with a STEM Lab in a box that contained only parent-donated materials. Within a year the materials filled a closet; and finally, with the enthusiasm and support of the school community, a STEM Lab was born. Sometimes shared challenges can inspire and engage support for the project.

As we mentioned in Chapter 4, partnerships are a crucial element in the success and sustainability of a STEM Lab. Not only do you want to think about current partnerships, but you should also look toward future ones as you build and grow your lab. These individuals, organizations, and/or businesses can provide financial support; they can also provide guidance and serve as a source for inspiration.

The next piece of the puzzle is the intersection of the STEM Lab and your curriculum. As the educational leader in the building, you will need to decide what grade levels will be utilizing the lab. This will vary from school to school depending on the grade span. In some educational settings, the use of the STEM Lab is limited to high performing students, gifted and talented students, or students in the upper grades. Our philosophy is an inclusive one. We believe that as many students as possible should have access to the STEM Lab, regardless of the grade, because all children can benefit from content-rich, authentic, hands-on exploration.

To lead the change process, you need to have a clear understanding of how the curriculum is being integrated within the STEM Lab and how the standards are being addressed. The key here is to encourage a "work smarter and not harder" environment, so that the teachers are not overwhelmed and turned off by the prospect of too much additional work. This is when common planning time plays a critical role. It is an opportunity to share ideas and address the issues related to project-based learning and STEM.

ISTE STANDARD
SYSTEMS DESIGNER

Leaders build teams and systems to implement, sustain and continually improve the use of technology to support learning. Education leaders:

4a. Lead teams to collaboratively establish robust infrastructure and systems needed to implement the strategic plan.

The STEM Lab is a venue for online research and technology use. One of the ways of cultivating responsible behavior online is to promote the school district's acceptable use policy and provide lessons on digital footprint.

ISTE STANDARD
EQUITY AND CITIZENSHIP ADVOCATE

Leaders use technology to increase equity, inclusion, and digital citizenship practices. Education leaders:

1a. Ensure all students have skilled teachers who actively use technology to meet students' learning needs.

1b. Ensure all students have access to the technology and connectivity necessary to participate in authentic and engaging learning opportunities.

1d. Cultivate responsible behavior online including the safe, ethical, and legal use of technology.

School leaders and technology coaches should ensure the technology infrastructure, equipment, and software in the school meets the needs of the students and teachers.

This is also a good time to provide support for your STEM teaching team by offering professional development opportunities. In preparation for PD, ask the teacher to answer these three questions:

1. *What do I know?* This question helps the teacher to acknowledge his/her strengths and prior knowledge.

2. *What do I need to learn?* This question initiates the development of a list of learning objectives that are personalized and meaningful for the individual.

3. *What is the best way for me to learn what I need to know?* This question recognizes that people learn in different ways.

This process encourages ownership and empowers the teacher to shape the content of the PD to his/her needs (Dirksen, 2012).

Once all of these key pieces are in place, you will want to ensure that the STEM Lab is being adequately utilized. What are your expectations in terms of the frequency of use? How will you ensure that there is equity and opportunity for all students? All other considerations aside, some teachers may feel a little intimidated by the lab and will hesitate to sign up. Others may want to take over the calendar and utilize the lab on a daily basis. It is very important to make sure that in addition to setting clear expectations, the school leaders monitor use of the lab, set boundaries where necessary, and provide support for teachers who are less confident in their use of the lab.

The caveat: Our recommendations are not foolproof and no two schools are the same. As a school leader, you are always trying to avoid roadblocks. What we can tell you is that by following the framework outlined above, you will be able to address some of the common challenges faced by school leaders who build STEM Labs. It helps to be ahead of the curve.

STEM LAB ADMINISTRATION 101

Here are a few of the practical, day-to-day management issues that may arise in the STEM Lab.

PREPARATION OF THE SPACE

Some schools hire designers or architects to prepare a blueprint for the makerspace. This is wise, particularly where walls are being removed and new wiring installed. In other cases, the school may be repurposing a classroom or shop room and the cleaning and prep is largely a collaboration between the administration, the custodial staff, and a volunteer workforce.

Dr. Janet Elder, is the principal of the Christa McAuliffe School, which serves a PK–8 student population. Elder's school has a very active STEM Lab that had humble beginnings. She describes the process like this:

> *For over 10 years I advocated for the transformation of a deserted woodshop into a STEM Lab. When they closed the middle school woodshop, they took the power tools and closed the door on a growing collection of junk. The room was used for storage of every kind of broken desk, discarded SMART board . . . any kind of junk that you can imagine. So one summer, we got together a great team—custodial and administrative—and we invested sweat equity to clean the room up and throw out stuff that had been down there for 25 years.*

When we finally got the room empty, the maintenance crew painted, put in new lights and ceiling tiles, and then I got a new floor in the next year after that. At that point I researched other labs in order to figure out what we should have in ours. So, when you come into our [STEM Lab] there are whiteboards all over the place; there are lounge areas with sofas for older kids; there is Wi-Fi, iPads, and [a] Mac desktop; there is an area for hand tools where students can make things with a hammer and nails; and there are workbenches. Of course, there are 3D printers, which are housed in a closet with a glass door. There is also an area for little kids, where there are Legos, Lincoln Logs, and things like that. (private conversation, May 2018)

Note, several of the school-based STEM Labs that we visited have a sink in the room. The sink—often a utility sink—is a convenient amenity for project preparation and cleanup. It is also, as Orly Nadler explained, an important safety tool for dealing with mishaps. When you are simply taking over a classroom, accessing a sink might not be possible. In that case, water and a bucket may be useful.

USE OF SPACE

How and how often you will use the lab is determined by the goals of the school and the curriculum. Some schools might use the lab daily, while others on an as-needed basis. Where most schools have one STEM Lab, the Northern Valley High School has two: one for design and prototyping, and the other for engineering and other projects that require power tools and machinery.

In the Christa McAuliffe school described above, every class has scheduled time in the lab each week for a science lesson. In addition, eight- or ten-week electives are scheduled, where the teachers create special STEM lessons and students at each grade level rotate through the lab working on the same activity. This is accomplished by condensing the other classes to free up a two-hour block for project-based learning.

Another example of balancing continuity of learning with use of the STEM Lab is described by Chani Lichtiger, the Technology Director of Yavneh Academy:

It used to be that every grade had a half-hour session, once a week and that was it. We moved away from that because I felt that it wasn't giving me the integration I was looking for. The younger students didn't remember what we did the week before. Now we try to see them a couple of times each week when we are working on a specific project.

SCHEDULING AND HOURS OF OPERATION

Before school, lunchtime, recess, after school, evenings, weekends, and summer programs are examples of the extracurricular timing for programs in the STEM Lab. The Christa McAuliffe school has a special program titled "Project Reservoir," in which select students in Grades 5 through 7 are invited to use the STEM Lab before school, beginning at 7:30 A.M., after school, and during the summer. Students in Project Reservoir submit projects for the Lexus Eco Challenge annually. In 2018, Christa McAuliffe students were the grand prize winners for middle school and were awarded $30,000.

Keep in mind that there needs to be faculty oversight whenever the lab is in use. Media specialists, for example, are not typically available for evening or weekend programs. Grant funding might be needed to cover the cost of personnel for special programs.

DOCUMENTING USE

There are three reasons that it is important to document use of the room:

➤ Responsibility for the equipment and materials in the room

➤ Documentation of use for the purpose of reports to board or funders

➤ A tool for creating future budgets (For example, it is helpful to know how much 3D printing filament is needed over a period of time.)

One simple example of documentation is a sign-up sheet outside of the door or Google calendar, where room availability is easily recognizable. This model, like the one used by Martha at A.D. Sullivan, is an informal, teacher-driven one. The lab is accessible to anyone who is interested in using it with their students.

Use of the 3D printer, laser cutter, table saws, drill presses, and other equipment may require a different kind of documentation. These types of machines are typically limited to use by certified instructors. In these instances, the sign-in sheet can include: name, date and time of use, a brief description of the project, approximate length of time needed. This information provides data for big picture analysis of the use of the lab and its equipment, allows the lab coordinator to help everyone complete projects in a timely fashion, and documents use in the case of injury or breakage.

The STEM Lab is home to expensive equipment, including laptops and tablets. Some schools currently use Radio Frequency Identification (RFID) technology to inventory and manage such equipment in their schools. David Rackliff, the IT Director for Emek Hebrew Day School, explains that he uses a system of bar code stickers called Asset Tags® for management of the school's inventory of laptops and that the same type of system is also applied to other types of equipment in the STEM Lab. Once the equipment is tagged and delivered to the lab, the coordinator who signs off on the receipt is responsible for it until inventory time the following summer.

SUPPLIES AND STORAGE

As you plan your STEM Lab, it is important to think about where you are going to keep tools, materials, and student projects, both incomplete and completed. Lockable cabinets, shelves, drawers, and bins are types of storage typically found in a STEM Lab. In many, a pegboard for storing hand tools is affixed to the wall above the electronics workbench. The objective is to keep the storage as unobtrusive as possible, making it easier to move furniture to the perimeter to accommodate different kinds of activities.

Preparation for completing a project in the STEM Lab means that the teacher needs to make sure that the correct materials are available in the necessary quantity. Lichtiger explains the process in her lab:

> *We have materials stored in a wall of cabinets. If teachers don't have what they need, they submit a list of materials that they will need in order to give choices to their students. Either we have the materials or we order them. If items are quite expensive, we ask the students if it is something that they wish to bring from home or if they can substitute something that is more affordable from our supplies. (private conversation, May 23, 2018)*

MAINTENANCE AND INSURANCE

As mentioned earlier, the custodial team is an important partner in a successful STEM Lab. Work together to create a plan for cleaning and maintaining the space. Where should student and teacher responsibility for cleanup end and maintenance's role begin?

Do your homework and invest the time in exploring warranty options. There are vendors that provide service contracts and are willing to repair or replace the equipment in the lab. This service may be either included with the warranty or available at an additional cost. Either way, it's certainly an option worth exploring. There is no point in having broken equipment in the STEM Lab because it defeats the purpose.

When one of Yavneh Academy's 3D printers broke down, the company sent a replacement motor, which they expected the school to install. No one in the lab felt qualified to do so. The lesson is that sometimes external expertise is needed to maintain the equipment in the lab. One option is to contact your local community makerspace. Makers are great sharers and can be a resource for technical talent and at least might be able to recommend where to find a good repair person.

STEM LAB STAFF

Someone needs to be the keeper of the keys, both in a practical sense, for the safety of the students and the security of your investment, and in the larger sense, as the responsible party or parties for the day-to-day operation of the STEM Lab.

There are a few reasons for this. First of all, school administrators do not have the time to manage (or micro-manage) the details of running the lab. Secondly, you are going to want to build capacity within your faculty and develop the sustainability of the lab.

You may want to begin with identifying a key person or a group of individuals that will assist in carrying out the vision for the lab. At the A.D. Sullivan School, a cadre of STEM leaders developed organically. This group consists of a math coach and several classroom teachers that are on staff. These individuals have taken ownership of the lab. They facilitate its use, provide peer-to-peer coaching, support project-based learning in the lab with team teaching, keep track of inventory, and ensure that the room is locked when not in use and that all expensive items are secure. They are also responsible for identifying items in need of repair and for notifying the administration when additional materials need to be ordered. The commitment of these individuals has been one of the biggest factors contributing to the success of the lab. Every school is unique and needs to work with available resources. While A.D. Sullivan school was fortunate enough to be able to depend upon a STEM team, other schools have seen equal success with one designated individual.

If you have a limited budget and restrictions regarding hiring personnel, you will need to think outside of the box. You may need to enlist the support of the media specialist, technology coach, math coach, or STEM coach to ensure that the lab is running smoothly. This kind of responsibility can foster leadership skills among faculty members. Again, the staffing needs of a high school STEM Lab, which truly emphasizes content and workplace readiness, are going to be different from that of an elementary or middle school. The bottom line on staffing your STEM Lab is to make it work. Be ready to use existing resources, look for grant funding or resources that can be supplied by partners, and make use of volunteers.

SAFETY AND SECURITY

Although learning goals are key, the safety and security of students are our primary responsibility while they are on campus and in the STEM Lab.

Students and faculty should be trained on the proper use of machinery and the safety rules for the lab. For example, where the use of certain power tools, such as saws or a laser cutter, are concerned, the school might require the use of safety goggles and that the students tie back long hair. Accidents should be reported to the STEM Lab coordinator and the school administration immediately using an incident report form (Figure 7.1). Your district may have a standard form that is recommended or required for use. Otherwise, check with district or school legal counsel before adopting a particular form for use.

EXAMPLE
PARKVIEW CENTRAL HIGH SCHOOL
STEM LAB INCIDENT FORM

INSTRUCTIONS: This form is to be completed by the STEM Lab Coordinator and submitted to a School Administrator.

Name of Individual(s) involved in the incident: _____

☐ Student ☐ Faculty ☐ Visitor ☐ Other _____

Date & Time of the incident: _____

If class was in session, what was the name of the class: _____

Location: _____

Describe the incident: (Was it due to illness, accident, or injury? If you answered accident or injury, please describe the exact circumstances and who was involved.)

_____

_____

_____

What steps were taken in response to the incident? (Did they involve contacting emergency personnel?)

_____

_____

_____

STEM LAB COORDINATOR	**ADMINISTRATOR**
Print Name _____	Print Name _____
Signature _____	Signature _____
Date _____	Date _____

FIGURE 7.1 Use an incident form to keep track of any accidents that occur in the STEM Lab. This form was created by the authors and is based on the forms used by Hampton University (science.hamptonu.edu/chem/docs/laboratoryIncident.pdf) and Columbia University (www.columbia.edu/cu/chemistry/pdf-files/Teaching_Lab_Incident_form.pdf).

STEM LAB STORY
MA'AYANOT YESHIVA HIGH SCHOOL FOR GIRLS, TEANECK, NEW JERSEY

Ma'ayanot is a small, private girls high school with a well-equipped and actively used STEM Lab (Figures 7.2 and 7.3). As described by Orly Nadler, Director of Technology, this STEM Lab began with a question:

> *How do we grow as a school? I was questioning whether we could continue to allow our students to opt out of the fundamental technological literacies that are at the heart of 21st century life. I banded together with the head of the Science Department, and together we sat down with the administration. We showed them about 20 newspaper articles [about STEAM education] and said: "This is happening. You can wait and allow the school to fall behind or if we do this right now, we can be pioneers and be the model school." They agreed. Kudos to the administration for really backing us up with unlimited funds and whatever we needed. (private conversation, May 14, 2018)*

Once the administration approved the STEM team's plan, the group took a year to think the project through and come up with a plan. Nadler did extensive research, visiting other schools and investigating the current STEAM research coming out of MIT. Nadler was adamant that STEAM, with the inclusion of Art, was the right direction for this girl's high school. As she explains:

> *Design aesthetics is at the core of what we do and the students love it. I wanted the students to be able to perceive technology as the ultimate tool for expression. To me the metrics of success was if the space will be populated with students even in off hours, like after school and during lunch. That is definitely the case.*

One of the most interesting things about the STEM Lab is its location, which is also a testament to the commitment of the school's leaders. The lab required a big space and the only option was the school library, so the library was transformed into a STEM Lab. The library books were moved to various locations throughout the building and another workspace was created for the students.

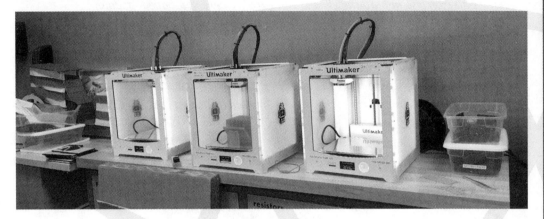

FIGURE 7.2 3D printers in the Ma'ayanot High School Stem Lab.

Nadler is committed to engaging everyone and making teachers, including non-STEM teachers, feel comfortable integrating the lab into their coursework. For example, she met with the school's English department and told them: "Listen we all have our specialties. I do not have yours, but I have my own. I feel very strongly that if we all bring what we are best at to the table, something awesome will come from the union of it." The result was a rich and meaningful lesson that combined the study of literature and botany. She adds: "If non-STEM teachers know that they are not expected to become engineers, they are a lot happier to work with you."

Nadler assesses project-based learning in the STEM Lab in the following way:

> I think that we've lost touch with educational theories of doing and we
> have to go back to Piaget's research. Creating projects in [the STEM Lab],
> by the nature of it, really levels the playing field. Anything that you're
> going to create demands much iteration and you don't know what the right
> answer is. Also working with an external artifact allows for success to be
> something that the individual can see and judge for themselves. I've never
> seen a student jumping for joy when she got a report card, but here, when
> she has worked on something and finally gets it right. It's unbelievable. The
> feeling of self-efficacy is a huge piece.

Nadler sees assessment as an ongoing process for herself, as well:

> *How do you demonstrate that the program is a success without making it an exercise in building Ikea [furniture], where you have to follow every single step? How do you create a structure that allows for different students to go at different speeds? I am constantly reflecting about how well something went and how it could be done differently and trying it out and iterating again. These are the same principles that we are trying to teach the students. This is the growth-oriented mindset that we want to see in our kids.*

FIGURE 7.3 The electronics tool bench in the Ma'ayanot High School Stem Lab.

COMPUTERS AND THE INTERNET

Following the trend in many other schools, the Immaculate Heart Academy in the Washington Township, New Jersey, has converted its library into a Learning Commons that includes a small lab featuring 3D printers. There are multiple computer stations in the library used for student research, as well as supporting the 3D printers. This type of arrangement, where media specialists play dual roles as library and lab supervisors, is becoming more and more common.

The use of computers and the internet for project research is to be anticipated; therefore digital citizenship is a topic of relevance to a STEM Lab. In an effort not to repeat information here that is readily available elsewhere, we will briefly mention the following:

➤ The school's acceptable use policy (AUP) also applies in the STEM Lab. The AUP is the set of rules for use of the internet and network on school computers, while on school property or outside of it. Teachers and staff are usually introduced to the AUP when they join the faculty.

➤ It is advisable to create a Student Code of Conduct for the lab. This would cover how students treat one another, the equipment, and work product within the STEM Lab. Appropriate behavior regarding digital citizenship is also a component of the Code of Conduct.

The district or school's director of technology, the technology coach, or local law enforcement officers are potential sources for training on issues of digital citizenship. Martha notes that the Business and Technology Department of her district is responsible for maintaining firewalls that limit access to sites that are not acceptable. A good resource for more information about digital citizenship is *Digital Citizenship in Action: Empowering Students to Engage in Online Communities*, by Kristen Mattson (ISTE, 2017). Another option is Google's Be Internet Awesome program (beinternetawesome.withgoogle.com/ en), which is a tool that can be taught by teachers in a many different disciplines. In this program, students "play their way to being internet Awesome with Interland, an online adventure that puts the key lessons of digital safety into hands-on practice with four challenging games" (Google, 2018). Multiple lessons are available for older students, including those published by Georgetown ISD (Commonsense Media, 2014).

ISTE STANDARD
EQUITY AND CITIZENSHIP ADVOCATE

Leaders use technology to increase equity, inclusion, and digital citizenship practices. Education leaders:

1d. Cultivate responsible online behavior, including the safe, ethical and legal use of technology.

School leaders can maintain a proactive approach by providing both students and parents with a variety of resources to promote responsible online behavior. Guest speakers, including law enforcement, can be invited to discuss a variety of topics including cyberbullying, digital footprint, and internet safety.

CHAPTER 7 RECAP

This chapter considered the administrative challenges involved in running a STEM Lab and offered a few tips for smooth running. Key points included:

➤ Administrative challenges in preparing and running a STEM Lab include preparation and maintenance of the physical plant. Flexibility is an important feature in a lab that needs to be able to accommodate many different kinds of activities.

➤ A designated person or small group should be assigned responsibility for oversight of the STEM Lab. The staff facilitates its use, including opening and closing; keeps track of sign-sheets or other documentation of usage; and serves as a point person(s) for identifying and informing the appropriate person about equipment that is in need of repair.

➤ Student safety and security within the lab is of the utmost importance. Faculty and students must be informed of the rules for working in the lab and must be trained on proper use of machinery.

This chapter described the mechanics for the day-to-day oversight and functioning of a STEM Lab. In Chapter 8, we will answer the most important questions: What does success look like? What does a STEM Lab contribute to a school and to its students?

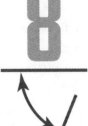

8 | IMPACT AND EXPECTATIONS

The goal is to get the students to take control of their own learning and say:

This was the challenge, these are the steps I took to accomplish it; this is my final product; and this is how I feel about it.

—MARCOS NAVAS,
TECHNOLOGY COORDINATOR, UNION CITY SCHOOLS,
UNION CITY, NEW JERSEY

DRIVING QUESTIONS

➤ What are the measures of success?

➤ What can a STEM Lab add to the STEM climate in a school?

➤ How can the STEM Lab empower student voice and choice?

STEM INTEGRATION WITHIN THE SCHOOL: BEFORE AND AFTER

This is a time of high stakes testing, when student success is measured by standardized assessment results. By contrast, project-based learning in the STEM Lab requires a different approach and is not one-size-fits-all. There are many ways to gather metrics in order to assess the progress of the students and the impact of the STEM Lab.

At one elementary school we learned that science, technology, and mathematics were taught in isolation across the grade levels. Once the school STEM Lab was launched, there was a shift in the expectations of the school leaders from teaching in silos to a more integrated approach. Documentation of lab use across grade levels was used as a measure of school improvement. Identifying who is using the lab and for what types of projects is another measure. For instance, is the lab seeing use from STEM classes and advanced classes only, or does use cut across the entire grade level and many different subject areas?

The number of STEM programs either before school or after school can also be an indicator of the lab's success. Many schools form clubs or teams that compete in state-wide or national STEM challenges. Documentation of the STEM Lab use in this type of project is another measure of progress. In some instances, the school also benefits from the prize award, which can contribute to the sustainability of the STEM Lab as well as the specific program.

Parent surveys are another tool for gathering data. Hillel School, for example, periodically polls its parents for feedback. These surveys include questions about the child's attitude toward learning in the STEM Lab and perceptions of the overall impact of project-based learning on the child.

Opportunities to work with institutions of higher education typically mean that the student or faculty member wishes to study some aspect of your school. Academic research is also an opportunity to gather data for evaluation. Documentary videos may be produced by the researcher as a portfolio addition or as a tool for recruiting grants. These videos can be used by the school as one form of documentation of the impact of the STEM program and lab.

STUDENT ASSESSMENT

Meghan McFerrin, Coordinator for the STEM/STEAM Georgia describes the school visits that take place in the STEM certification process as focusing on the engagement and work product of the students: "We want to see student ownership, that students understand what they're learning." The department uses a rubric to assess schools at different levels and in all cases the school has to demonstrate that they have provided students with opportunities to show and explain their STEM projects. Often schools in Georgia, and elsewhere, will host a STEM/STEAM fair or a Maker Faire, where student projects are displayed exhibition-style. Family, faculty, community members, and local business leaders are invited to attend and listen to presentations by individual students.

Making is another description for the creative process that takes place in the STEM Lab. The overlap between school-based makerspaces and STEM Labs in education is significant. Both feature essentially three types of projects:

1. Projects that are the result of direct instruction by the teacher. An example would be instructions on how to safely use machines or learning about the design thinking process;

2. Projects that are guided, where the student replicates someone else's work. An example would be following instructions in order to build a kit or recreate a project that was done by the students in a previous year; and

3. Projects that are devised and produced by the student. An example would be an original capstone project. (Dougherty, 2016)

Whether the student is learning how to use tools and follow directions, or is engaged in a multi-step design process, the result is tangible. Projects create products, and these products are an important tool for assessing student work in a STEM Lab. Dale Dougherty, the founder of *Make:* magazine and MakerEd.org, explains:

> *Making is its own form of assessment for authentic learning. The products of making demonstrate what a person can do, and what they know. The process itself and the steps along the way can be observed, reported on, reflected upon, and documented in various ways and in various formats (2016, p. 195).*

The students' STEM Lab work product can be gathered into an open portfolio system that is very effective for assessing project-based learning. An example can be found on the MakerEd website. As Marcos Navas, Technology Director for the Union City, New Jersey, schools describes an open portfolio, its key features are that it is performance based, it is rubric based, and it measures growth by asking the students to document their work. Students also learn how to create and edit videos and pictures while documenting.

The MakerEd.org Open Portfolio rubric maps the student's journey as he/she processes a work product, while reflecting and collecting data along the way (Documentation of learning, n.a.). The rubric describes four steps that are used in this process:

➤ **CAPTURE:** the student documents learning using digital and analog tools (e.g. audio, video, print, drawings);

➤ **COLLECT:** the student stores "digital assets" in the cloud;

➤ **CURATE:** the student organizes the materials into a "coherent narrative" (e.g. blog post, video, online portfolio, or photo album); and

➤ **SHARE:** the student shares the portfolio with the public.

(Documentation of learning, n.a., para.1–4)

The goal of the Open Portfolio is to enable the student to capture the process and product of their work, reflect upon it, and then share it with the class.

Many colleges, including the top-tier ones such as MIT, accept portfolios as a part of the application process (Dougherty, 2016). The portfolio development process, therefore, is another way to develop the young learner's sense of agency over his/her path to higher education and employment. With the accessibility of video and audio recording tools, as well as the growing capacity of mobile devices, the digital divide has less impact on portfolio preparation.

CULTIVATING A STEM CLIMATE

The thoughtful planning and implementation of a STEM Lab can have a profound impact on the climate of the school, especially if the leadership has vision and passion, and empowers the key players. When all stakeholders have a vested interest in the success of the STEM Lab, it is more likely to succeed and thrive. As Meghan McCullen describes it, the move to create a STEM climate in the school "has to come from an authentic place and a place of integrity, of wanting to do what's best for students and to change your school instruction on the student's behalf."

When your efforts are a success, you'll see it reflected in your students. According to Steve Freedman of the Hillel Day School, "Success looks like students who are engaged, actively learning, lose sight of the time, and can reflect on their experience. If you measure it against the mission: students are inspired to learn."

How does a STEM climate come to be? The STEM Lab focuses the spotlight on interdisciplinary content, which challenges the traditional siloed approach of the 20th century. It makes an audacious statement that real life is not compartmentalized, so neither should education be. The STEM Lab opens the door to authentic learning that is immersive and meaningful. This is another challenge to the status quo, especially because it is engaging the students and changing their expectations of what learning should look like. The STEM Lab supports project-based learning that is hands-on and inquiry-based. It is the place where a school's commitment to growth mindset is put to the test. The process of teach, review, test, and then standardized test does not teach agency, self-reliance, or the role of failure in success. Whereas the design thinking process, with its iterative attempts until a successful result has been achieved, is a true platform for the development of a growth mindset.

In sum, the STEM Lab can help transform the culture of learning in a school and the perceptions of learning for the individual and the community. McCullen relates the following story. Principals in schools with Georgia STEM certification are reporting a decline in discipline issues and a rise in attendance because students are so engaged and there is a positive school culture. One day, however, McCullen was on a site visit to a STEM-certified school and she noticed that a little boy was acting out. The teacher was embarrassed and so McCullen asked: "What's wrong? Why is he upset?" The teacher replied: "Oh, he doesn't want to leave class. We are building a roller coaster and he doesn't want to stop what he is doing. The kids are so excited and want to learn more, and it's really contagious all over the school." Janet Elder sums up the efficacy of the STEM Lab: "There are two parts to my philosophy of education: If we can teach you to read, we can teach you to learn, and if we have a hook, you have a reason why you want to be in school" (private conversation, May 15, 2018). A STEM Lab can be that hook.

STEM LAB STORY
UNION CITY SCHOOL DISTRICT, UNION CITY, NEW JERSEY

For the public schools in Union City, the path to opening STEM Labs was a gradual one. Five years ago, they started introducing some STEM concepts and doing some experiments with small STEM camps of 40 or 60 kids. The students had a very positive reaction and enjoyed the inquiry and the science side of the program. The integration of the technology also met with success, so the following year they decided to grow the program a little bit more.

From there Marcos Navas, the STEM coordinator for the district, started offering STEM PD for teachers. He describes it as an integrated approach that talks about growth mindset and fosters the idea of student-centered classes. He has found that teachers are receptive to this approach.

Next, Navas began visiting selected schools in the district and working with small teams to start integrating STEM into the day-to-day classwork of the students. As he describes the process, "It started with little pockets of interest and then as the requests for STEM kept growing, we kept just building on the momentum" (interview, May 23, 2018).

Eventually, STEM began to capture the attention of Union City's school leaders. They started to come to Navas asking questions about STEM Labs. One of the principals was extremely impressed by the excitement of the students coming back to school after STEM summer camp. She decided to capitalize on that energy for ongoing learning by building an entire STEM floor in her school. So far, the floor contains a STEM Lab, a hydroponics room, and a video-editing space.

From its small beginning, with pockets of integration, the STEM program in Union City has grown exponentially to include STEM Labs in multiple schools. "Most of these STEM Labs were grant-funded," Navas adds, "but in some cases the school was willing to separate some of their own funding to make this idea happen. I believe that once someone sees the value of a certain area, the value of certain tools that you are investing in, I think it just becomes a natural part of the budget and ecosystem."

How does Navas capture the successes of the STEM program and STEM Labs in Union City?

I measure success in a couple of different ways, I've been looking at the open portfolio system, which you can find on the MakerEd website. It's perfor-mance-based and rubric-based. It is definitely a means of measuring growth by looking at the process we use to get through the challenge or reach a goal. It is totally different from [the system] we currently use: Monday, introduce the idea; three days of worksheets; and then a test on Friday.

Because it is so student-centered, the interest in STEM comes at a perfect time in education. We're coming to a time where we see the necessity for change. We see that the old ways of teaching are not helping today's digital students. So, we're working at STEM as a way to introduce this new model of education where students are at the center. Their voice is valued, their ideas and personal opinions are valued.

It's a very different world from the traditional teacher-centered class-room. So, STEM is at this perfect boom in education, at this burst of change. I see STEM as one of those catalysts taking us into the future.

> ## ISTE STANDARD
> ## EMPOWERING LEADER
>
> Leaders create a culture where teachers and learners are empowered to use technology in innovative ways to enrich teaching and learning. Education leaders:
>
> 3c. Inspire a culture of innovation and collaboration that allows the time and space to explore and experiment with digital tools.
>
> Project-based learning and design thinking in the STEM Lab promote collaboration and innovation. STEM competitions and engineering or design challenges can empower the learners to utilize technology while promoting team-building skills.

STUDENT VOICE AND CHOICE

What do we mean by student voice and choice? Student voice means that the ideas and opinions of the students are requested and welcomed. Student choice means that the students can choose between different learning pathways or projects. Together, they form the basis for co-construction of knowledge between the student and the teacher (Alber, 2014). In this approach, the teacher and the student are both learners.

The teacher cedes some instructional authority to make room for growth and exploration by the student. When the teacher gives up total control over the boundaries of study, learning can move into uncharted territory. The teacher may need to admit that he/she doesn't know the answer. This is a frightening prospect for some. The teacher's next response is pivotal: Why don't we try to find out together? Here the teacher is providing the student with a valuable lesson. When faced with the unknown, find a way to learn about it and make it known.

Student voice and choice are core principles in project-based learning (Niehof, 2017). Amplifying student voice can enhance social and emotional learning by empowering students, promoting self-expression, and critical thinking. One of the technology tools that we use to encourage student voice is Flipgrid, a user-friendly app that allows the students to record brief video responses using mobile devices. It provides students with an opportunity to demonstrate their learning while giving teachers a tool to assess student progress.

ISTE AND STUDENT VOICE

ISTE encourages student participation in its conferences. The poster sessions offer a rich opportunity for students to present and interact informally with other conference attendees. During the 2014–15 school year, Deborah led an after-school maker program at the Urban Assembly Maker Academy, a career technical high school in New York City. The group's primary project was to create a documentary film about the school. From the initial film concept and story-boarding through final editing, these ninth-grade students were responsible for producing and directing the film. In the summer of 2015, she brought the film and a dozen students to present at one of the 15 ISTE poster sessions. Prior to the conference, she worked with them on presentation skills, and they mapped out the types of conversations they would have with interested attendees. The students shone at the poster session, demonstrating tremendous poise and self-confidence while interacting with professional educators at the conference. As an added bonus, they were inspired by what they saw at ISTE: a community committed to the use of design and technology in ways that mirrored their own project-based learning in the high school.

PROMOTING STUDENT CHOICE

There are many different ways that teachers can encourage student choice in the STEM Lab. Students can be invited to:

➤ Choose between a selection of problems.

➤ Determine what kinds of materials they will use to solve the problem.

➤ Select the group of students with which they will work.

➤ Decide which tools they will use to collect data.

Creativity, self-reliance, critical thinking, communication and collaboration skills, and an innovative spirit are among the most recognized qualifications for the 21st century workforce (Niehof, 2017). Opportunities for choice at school help students to develop these skills in a safe and supporting environment.

According to Tikvah Wiener, when you promote student voice and choice you are asking students "to explore their natural strengths." Essentially, you are asking them to answer the questions: "What strengths do I have, and how am I going to use them to make a better world?" If students are asked to address a real-world problem, say social justice for a particular group of people, they can choose different ways of approaching the solution. One student might create a social awareness campaign, and the other might go into the STEAM Lab and create a physical solution to address the problem. Each student needs to find what is most meaningful for himself or herself. Both approaches are valuable.

CHAPTER 8 RECAP

A successful STEM Lab is planned and built with vision and goals in mind. As with any innovation, there comes a point when you ask: Have I achieved my goals? This chapter discussed some measure of success and other indicators that the STEM Lab has had an impact on the school. Key points included:

➤ Measures of success can be found in data regarding frequency of use of the STEM Lab, who uses the STEM Lab, what types of projects are produced there, and how well STEM Lab work is integrated into the rest of the STEM curriculum.

➤ A successful STEM Lab can enhance the school climate by inspiring enthusiasm, curiosity, and self-efficacy in the students.

➤ The STEM Lab activity offers singular opportunities for student voice and choice because it engages students in solving real-world problems using a multi-step design process where no two solutions are alike. Not only must students choose which steps to take, but they also have the opportunity to share their process and end product with others.

Just like the projects that take shape within the STEM Lab, the STEM Lab itself is a product of a design process. In every design process, the prototype is tested and evaluated. This is not the end of the process, but the beginning of a new iteration where the design is improved based on data assessment, feedback, and realignment with your goals.

FINAL THOUGHTS

In the pages of this book, you have met school leaders in urban, suburban, and rural schools with classes K–8, PK–5, and high school. You have heard about a variety of STEM Labs: from the ground floor stages of development to a visionary reconstruction of a STEM Learning Hub for project-based learning. You have seen STEM Labs made from repurposed classrooms, reimagined media centers, and regional resources. STEM Labs come in all shapes and sizes. Every school, every community must find the right fit.

For the more than two-dozen interviews and conversations that provided the foundation for this book, we asked these school leaders to look in the mirror and describe their STEM programs and the role of the STEM Lab in realizing their visions.

We heard them say:

➤ Start with a clear vision and continually measure your choices against your vision.

➤ Bringing your stakeholders on board is an iterative process.

➤ Teachers are the most important variables in the STEM Lab equation, so professional development is key.

➤ Plan with your students in mind, and let the principles of Universal Design for Learning (UDL), such as voice and choice, be your guide.

➤ Stay alert for opportunities because partnerships, financial support, and many different sources of PD are everywhere.

➤ Don't be afraid to start small and build in stages.

At the beginning of this book, we offered a simple recipe for success: Idea + Passion + Opportunity. Of course, as you might have expected, building a successful STEM Lab is anything but simple. The idea must be a clear and consistent vision that will stand the test of feedback and hundreds of reiterations as it is used to enroll supporters. This vision is the basis for a complete plan with action goals and benchmarks for evaluation.

Passion only begins to describe the depth of commitment and resilience that are needed to successfully orchestrate the symphony of technology, methodology, and content in the STEM Lab. Opportunity is not a large enough word to capture the volume and variety of potential partners, funders, service providers, and sources for programs and PD that you will find with effort and an entrepreneurial spirit.

Just because no one in your school or district has tried or succeeded at building a STEM Lab, it doesn't mean that it is not possible. This is the moment of STEM. Educational technology has overtaken blackboards and textbooks. It is a world where our students want to learn how to be producers, rather than passive consumers. It is a time of access to vast knowledge on the internet, where, for our students, STEM is not just about a job in their future but also about connecting with the emerging technologies of everyday life.

STEAM Lab, Makerspace, Fab Lab, Creativity Commons, Imagination Hub—there are a hundred names for STEM Labs, each one reflecting different facets of the vision of their builders. We audaciously gathered all of these environments under one umbrella term for the sake of convenience and to make a point. All of these labs share the common essence that was presented by Tikvah Wiener in Chapter 1: It is about the head, the heart, and the hands. Here is how we explain it:

A STEM LAB IS NOT JUST A SPACE. It a reflection of a mindset that focuses attention on STEM education and shows dedication to preparing our students for college, a changing workplace, and a technology-driven life.

IT IS A LOCUS FOR EDUCATIONAL CHANGE. Our students are looking for authentic education. They want to learn about and design solutions for real-world problems. The interdisciplinary content, inquiry-based approach, and design-thinking tools of the STEM Lab are an invitation for our students to learn with their hearts.

IT IS AN OPPORTUNITY TO REINVENT EDUCATION. The factory model of education that served us during the first Industrial Revolution cannot meet the demands of the digital age. Project-based learning, by contrast, is hands-on, personalized, and invites creativity and innovation. The STEM Lab is a venue for learning by doing, rather than learning by listening and retelling.

If this book has reinforced your vision of STEM education and STEM Labs—or raised questions about how you can improve some aspect of your work with STEM education and STEM Labs, or planted even the smallest seed of the idea that your district or school should give more thought to the role of STEM education and STEM

Labs—then you are part of the movement. We invite you to nurture your idea through research and conversation with other school leaders working in STEM education. We encourage you to fuel your passion and use it inspire others around you to join in the reinvention of education. We thank all of the contributors to this book for their candor and insights. And, we hope that their examples will empower you to plug yourself and your school or district into the amazing opportunities that are available to support your STEM vision and STEM Lab.

APPENDIX A
ISTE STANDARDS FOR EDUCATION LEADERS

STANDARD 1: EQUITY AND CITIZENSHIP ADVOCATE

Leaders use technology to increase equity, inclusion, and digital citizenship practices. Education leaders:

a. Ensure all students have skilled teachers who actively use technology to meet student learning needs.

b. Ensure all students have access to the technology and connectivity necessary to participate in authentic and engaging learning opportunities.

c. Model digital citizenship by critically evaluating online resources, engaging in civil discourse online and using digital tools to contribute to positive social change.

d. Cultivate responsible online behavior, including the safe, ethical and legal use of technology.

STANDARD 2: VISIONARY PLANNER

Leaders engage others in establishing a vision, strategic plan and ongoing evaluation cycle for transforming learning with technology. Education leaders:

a. Engage education stakeholders in developing and adopting a shared vision for using technology to improve student success, informed by the learning sciences.

b. Build on the shared vision by collaboratively creating a strategic plan that articulates how technology will be used to enhance learning.

c. Evaluate progress on the strategic plan, make course corrections, measure impact and scale effective approaches for using technology to transform learning.

d. Communicate effectively with stakeholders to gather input on the plan, celebrate successes and engage in a continuous improvement cycle.

e. Share lessons learned, best practices, challenges and the impact of learning with technology with other education leaders who want to learn from this work.

STANDARD 3: EMPOWERING LEADER

Leaders create a culture where teachers and learners are empowered to use technology in innovative ways to enrich teaching and learning. Education leaders:

a. Empower educators to exercise professional agency, build teacher leadership skills and pursue personalized professional learning.

b. Build the confidence and competency of educators to put the ISTE Standards for Students and Educators into practice.

c. Inspire a culture of innovation and collaboration that allows the time and space to explore and experiment with digital tools.

d. Support educators in using technology to advance learning that meets the diverse learning, cultural, and social-emotional needs of individual students.

e. Develop learning assessments that provide a personalized, actionable view of student progress in real time.

STANDARD 4: SYSTEMS DESIGNER

Leaders build teams and systems to implement, sustain and continually improve the use of technology to support learning. Education leaders:

a. Lead teams to collaboratively establish robust infrastructure and systems needed to implement the strategic plan.

b. Ensure that resources for supporting the effective use of technology for learning are sufficient and scalable to meet future demand.

c. Protect privacy and security by ensuring that students and staff observe effective privacy and data management policies.

d. Establish partnerships that support the strategic vision, achieve learning priorities and improve operations.

STANDARD 5: CONNECTED LEARNER

Leaders model and promote continuous professional learning for themselves and others. Education leaders:

a. Set goals to remain current on emerging technologies for learning, innovations in pedagogy and advancements in the learning sciences.

b. Participate regularly in online professional learning networks to collaboratively learn with and mentor other professionals.

c. Use technology to regularly engage in reflective practices that support personal and professional growth.

d. Develop the skills needed to lead and navigate change, advance systems and promote a mindset of continuous improvement for how technology can improve learning.

APPENDIX B
RESOURCES

Here is a list of resources to help you in establishing and managing your STEM Lab. We hope you find them as helpful as we have!

STANDARDS, CURRICULUM, AND METHODOLOGY

The STEM Lab's connections to standards and curriculum, as well as its foundations in project-based learning, are defining features of this approach to STEM education.

Buck Institute for Education offers professional development services on how to develop and implement project-based learning. http://www.bie.org

The following publications present examples of both project-based learning and inter-disciplinary study that are applicable in a STEM Lab:

➤ *STEM Project-Based Learning: An Integrated Science, Technology, Engineering, and Mathematics (STEM) Approach.* Capraro, R. M., Capraro, M. M., & Morgan, J. R. (Eds.). (2013). Boston, MA: Sense Publishers.

➤ **"Six Characteristics of a Great STEM Lesson."** Jolly, A. (2014, June 17). *Education Week.* https://tinyurl.com/ybznrhrx

➤ **"What Are the Benefits of Interdisciplinary Study?"** Open University. (2015, April 9). Open Learn: Education & Development. http://www.open.edu/openlearn/education/what-are-the-benefits-interdisciplinary-study

Pinterest is an online pinboard or social bookmarking site that features linked images from web pages. Subscribers collect these images on their boards. There are nearly 1,000 STEM-related boards on Pinterest. www.pinterest.com

Teachers Pay Teachers is an online educational marketplace, where educators share lesson plans and other resources. Teacher-tested materials for STEM projects are available there. https://www.teacherspayteachers.com

The New Jersey Student Learning Standards provide academic standards, benchmarks, and student achievement in nine content areas for students in PK–12. https://www.nj.gov/education/cccs

The Maryland State STEM Standards of Practice provide a framework for Grades K–12. School Improvement in Maryland. http://mdk12.msde.maryland.gov/instruction/curriculum/stem

STEM

The Latinas in STEM Foundation is a nonprofit organization designed to encourage Latinas to pursue and thrive in STEM fields. This organization provides K–12 community outreach, professional development, and opportunities for college students. http://www.latinasinstem.com

The *Latinas in STEM 101 Conference* **video** shows the premiere of the STEM 101 Conference sponsored by the Latinas in STEM Foundation and hosted at Alexander D. Sullivan School. It provides a snapshot of the many elements involved in setting up a STEM Conference. Latinas in STEM 101 Conference (2016, March 26). STEM 101 Conference. https://youtu.be/n-nyfnsdPOc

Liberty Science Center is an example of a regional science museum that offers student field trips, school visits, specialized STEM activities (e.g., the *Live From Surgery* program), professional development, and a STEM education guide. https://lsc.org

The article, "**Science, Technology, Engineering & Mathematics Resources for preK-12**," offers a selection of STEM tools and lesson plans compiled by the National Education Association. Nast, P. (2017). National Education Association. http://www.nea.org/tools/lessons/stem-resources.html

Science Buddies provides a variety of STEM project kits for purchase, as well as offering science fair project ideas and a repository of free STEM lessons. https://www.sciencebuddies.org

The Society of Women Engineers is a professional and collegiate organization that provides learning opportunities, grants, scholarships, and K–12 community outreach. http://societyofwomenengineers.swe.org

ASSESSMENT

The following two articles offer examples of assessment in the context of project-based learning.

➤ **"Project-Based Learning for the 21st Century: Skills for the Future."** Bell, S. (2010, July 8). *The Clearing House: A Journal of Educational Strategies, Ideas and Issues.* https://www.tandfonline.com/doi/full/10.1080/00098650903505415

➤ **"Assessment of Project-Based Learning in a MECHTRONICS Context."** Doppelt, Y. (2005). *Journal of Educational Technology, 12*(2)2-24. https://files.eric.ed.gov/fulltext/EJ1063599.pdf

Flipgrid is an online resource whereby students can easily video record responses to teacher-directed assessments. This is an example of a tool that can be used to amplify student voice. https://www.flipgrid.com

MakerEd Open Portfolio combines research and practice to develop a common framework for documenting, sharing, and assessing learning through portfolios. http://makered.org/opp

PROFESSIONAL DEVELOPMENT

The book *Handbook of Technological Pedagogical Content Knowledge (TPACK) for Educators* (2nd Ed.) is a primer for developing training in the context of TPACK. Herring, M. C., Koehler, M. J., & Mishra, P. (Eds.). (2016). New York, New York: Routledge.

3D PRINTING

3D printing is a fun and challenging way to engage your students in design thinking. Here are a few basic tools and resources in this growing area of interest.

Enabling the Future is a global community designed to aid with the 3D printing of open-source prosthetics. http://enablingthefuture.org

MakerBot Thingiverse provides users with the ability to design and share 3D models and 3D scanners with others within the community. https://www.thingiverse.com

Pico Turbine International provides 3D tech support, professional development, and a STEM curriculum. http://www.picoturbine.com

Tinkercad is an open-source app that can be used by students, teachers, and tinkerers for the purpose of designing 3D electronics and coding. https://www.tinkercad.com

CODING

Coding is an important skill for students who employ technology in 3D printing, robotics, electronics, and other STEM Lab activities. These resources are examples of organizations and websites that support learners engaged in coding.

CoderDojo is a global and local community of volunteers to support young learners in developing coding skills. https://coderdojo.com

Code.org is a nonprofit organization designed to support the implementation of computer science in Grades K–12. This resource provides a computer science curriculum, tutorials, and online resources for both students and teachers. https://code.org

Girls Who Code is an organization designed to build a pipeline of female engineers by providing a series of computer science programs for girls in Grades 3–12. https://girlswhocode.com

Made w/ Code provides a variety of coding projects, partner projects, and coding events. https://www.madewithcode.com

ENGINEERING

Engineering activities are at the core of STEM. A wide variety of resources are available on the internet. Here are two that have played an important role in our STEM Lab.

Engineering is Elementary is developed by the Museum of Science, Boston. EiE provides professional development opportunities, as well as an engineering curriculum for young learners. https://www.eie.org

Society of Hispanic Professional Engineers offers K–12 outreach and scholarship opportunities, as well as local and regional events. http://www.shpe.org

ADMINISTRATION

One consideration in the day-to-day administration of a STEM Lab is safety and security, as is highlighted in the article below.

"Safety and Liability in STEM Education Laboratories: Using Case Law to Inform Policy and Practice." Dove, T. S. (2014, February). *Technology and Engineering Teacher, 73* (5), 1-7) https://www.iteea.org/File.aspx?id=47091&v=7a8cac88

The *STEM 2026: A Cision for Innovation in STEM Education* report, by the U.S. Department of Education, gives an overview of the most important elements of a vision for STEM education. U.S. Department of Education, Office of Innovation and Improvement. (2016). Washington, DC.

REFERENCES

Alber, R. (2014, March 3). 5 ways to give your students more voice and choice. *Edutopia*. Retrieved from https://www.edutopia.org/blog/five-strategies-more-voice-choice-students-rebecca-alber

Barron, B., et al., (1998). Doing with understanding: Lessons from research on problem-based and project-based learning. *The Journal of the Learning Sciences, 7*(3–4), 271–311.

Barshay, J. (2016, December 6). U.S. now ranks near the bottom among 35 industrialized nations in math. *The Hechinger Report*. Retrieved from https://hechingerreport.org/u-s-now-ranks-near-bottom-among-35-industrialized-nations-math

Bennett, A. (2014, December). Project-based science: A pathway to problem-solving skills. *Children's Technology and Engineering, 19*(2), 20–24. Retrieved from https://www.questia.com/magazine/1G1-403918328/project-based-science-a-pathway-to-problem-solving

Brett, J. (2017, July 27). Coming soon to a high school near you: The Georgia film academy. Atlanta Buzz, Cox Media Group. Retrieved from https://www.ajc.com/blog/buzz/coming-soon-high-school-near-you-the-georgia-film-academy/WNxlVyxaeSZ3XUicqQQMEJ

Bruner, J. (1966). *Toward a theory of instruction*. Cambridge, MA: Harvard University Press. p. 69.

Bureau of Labor Statistics. (2018, January 30). Employment projections 2016–2026 [PDF file]. Retrieved from https://www.bls.gov/news.release/archives/ecopro_10242017.pdf

Committee on Prospering in the Global Economy of the 21st Century (U.S.), & Committee on Science, Engineering, and Public Policy (U.S.). (2007). *Rising above the gathering storm: Energizing and employing America for a brighter economic future*. Washington, D.C: National Academies Press.

Chute, E. (2009, February 10). STEM education is branching out: Focus shifts from making science, math accessible to more than just brightest. *Pittsburgh Post-Gazette*. Retrieved from http://www.post-gazette.com/pg/09041/947944-298.stm

College of Engineering, University of Colorado. (2017). Curricular unit: Bridges. *Teach Engineering: STEM Curriculum for k-12*. Retrieved from https://www.teachengineering.org/curricularunits/view/cub_brid_curricularunit

DeSilver, D. (2017, February 15). U.S. students' academic achievement still lags that of their peers in many other countries. *Pew Research Center*. Retrieved from http://www.pewresearch.org/fact-tank/2017/02/15/u-s-students-internationally-math-science

Dirksen. J. (2012). *Design for how people learn*. Berkeley, CA: New Riders.

Documentation of learning. (n.a.). Open portfolios: Journey map [PDF file]. Retrieved from http://makered.org/wp-content/uploads/2018/02/MakerEdOPP_JourneyMap_final.pdf

Dominey, C. (2018). Film industry in Georgia. *New Georgia Encyclopedia*. Retrieved from https://www.georgiaencyclopedia.org/articles/arts-culture/film-industry-georgia

Doran, G. T. (1981). There's a S.M.A.R.T. way to write management's goals and objectives. *Management Review, 70*, 35–36.

Dougherty, D. (2016). *Free to make: How the maker movement is changing our schools, our jobs, and our minds*. Berkeley, CA: North Atlantic Books.

Dweck, C. (2009, November/December). Who will the 21st-century learners be? *Knowledge Quest. 38*(2), 8–9.

Ebarb. M. (2018, January 12). Full STEAM ahead: Headquarters directorate partners with area schools to enhance students' knowledge. Education, Museum of Aviation Foundation. Retrieved from http://www.museumofaviation.org/2018/01/12/full-steam-ahead-headquarters-directorate-partners-area-schools-enhance-students-knowledge

Effective Partnerships. (2014). Principles of effective partnerships [PDF file]. National Center for Community Schools. Retrieved from http://www.csstrategies.org/wp-content/uploads/2016/05/Principles-of-Effective-Partnerships.pdf

Empowering a New Generation. (2018). Panasonic creative design challenge. Panasonic. Retrieved from https://na.panasonic.com/us/CDC

Fleming, L. (2015). *Worlds of making: Best practices for establishing a makerspace for your school.* Thousand Oaks, CA: Corwin.

Freeport School District. (2007). Freeport school district plan on a page. Retrieved from http://www.ascd.org/ASCD/pdf/el/Reeves%20Plan.pdf

Fried, D. (2018, May 4). *Biochemistry literacy for kids documentary* [Video]. Retrieved from https://www.youtube.com/watch?v=qflUTYv67e4

Fullan, M. (2016). *The new meaning of educational change.* New York, NY: Teachers College Press.

Georgetown Independent School District. (n.a.). Digital citizenship lessons for students. Retrieved from https://www.georgetownisd.org/digitalcitizenship

Georgia DOE. (n.a.). STEM business/community/post-secondary partnership levels [PDF file]. *STEM Georgia STEAM Georgia.* Retrieved from http://www.stemgeorgia.org/certification

Goodson, I., Moore, S., & Hargreaves, A. (2006). Teacher nostalgia and the sustainability of reform: The generation and degeneration of teachers' missions, memory and meaning. *Educational Administration Quarterly, 42*(1), 42–61.

High Tech High. (2018). About High Tech High. Retrieved from https://www.hightechhigh.org/about-us

Hochanadel, A. & Finamore, D. (2015). Fixed and growth mindset in education and how grit helps students persist in the face of adversity. *Journal of International Education Research, 11*(1), 47–50.

International Society for Technology in Education. *ISTE Standards for Education Leaders* (2018). Retrieved from https://www.iste.org/standards/for-education-leaders

Koehler, M. J., Shin, T. S., & Mishra, P. (2012). How do we measure TPACK? Let me count the ways. In R. N. Ronau, C. R. Rakes, & M. L. Niess (Eds.), *Educational technology, teacher knowledge, and classroom impact: A research handbook on frameworks and approaches* (pp. 16-31). Hershey, PA: IGI Global.

Leithwood, K. & Seashore Louis, K. (2012). *Linking leadership to student learning*. San Francisco, CA: Jossey-Bass.

Lou, N. & Peek, K. (2016, February 23). By the numbers: The rise of the makerspace. *Popular Science*. Retrieved from http://www.popsci.com/rise-makerspace-by-numbers

Lynch, M. (2016). Three important critiques of standardized assessments [Blog]. *Education Week*. Retrieved from http://blogs.edweek.org/edweek/education_futures/2016/06/three_important_critiques_of_standardized_assessments.html

Martinez, S. L. & Stager, G. (2013). *Invent to learn: Making, tinkering, and engineering in the classroom*. Torrance, CA: Constructing Modern Knowledge Press.

Mindset Works. (2017). Understanding mindsets. Fixed vs. growth: Understand the two basic mindsets that shape our lives. Retrieved from https://www.mindsetworks.com/parents/understanding-mindset

NCTM. (2018). Principles and standards for school mathematics. Retrieved from https://www.nctm.org/Standards-and-Positions/Principles-and-Standards

NGSS Lead States. (2013). Next generation science standards: For states, by states. Retrieved from http://www.nextgenscience.org/trademark-and-copyright

Niehoff, M. (2017, April 12). Student voice and choice: It's not just for projects anymore [Blog post]. Buck Institute for Education, PBL. Retrieved from https://www.bie.org/blog/student_voice_and_choice_its_not_just_for_projects_anymore

Northouse, P. (2013). *Leadership: Theory and practice*, 6th edition. Thousand Oaks, CA: Sage.

Our knowledge-based economy. (n.a.). Why was the STEM education caucus created? STEMEd Caucus Steering Committee. Retrieved from http://nstacommunities.org/stemedcaucus

Papert, S. (1993). *Mindstorms: Children, computers, and powerful ideas*. New York, NY: Basic Books.

Partnership for 21st Century Learning. (2018). Framework for 21st century learning. Retrieved from http://www.p21.org/our-work/p21-framework

Principles of Effective Partnerships. (n.a.). Principles of effective partnerships [PDF file]. The Whole Child. Retrieved from http://www.wholechildeducation.org/assets/content/mx-resources/handoutprinciplespartnership.pdf

Problem Solving. (2018). Process. *National Council of Teachers of Mathematics*. Retrieved from https://www.nctm.org/Standards-and-Positions/Principles-and-Standards/Process

Reeves, D.B. (2008). Leading to change: Making strategic planning work. *Educational Leadership: Informative Assessment*, pp. 86–87.

Sampson, A.V. (2016, September). Rural Education. *New Georgia Encyclopedia*. Retrieved from https://www.georgiaencyclopedia.org/articles/education/rural-education

Sivers, D. (2010, February 11). First follower: Leadership lesson from a dancing guy. [Video file]. Sivers.org. Retrieved from https://www.ted.com/talks/derek_sivers_how_to_start_a_movement/up-next

Snyder, R.R. (2017). Resistance to change among veteran teachers: Providing voice for more effective engagement [PDF file]. *NCPEA International Journal of Educational Leadership Preparation, 21*(1), pp.1-14. Retrieved from https://files.eric.ed.gov/fulltext/EJ1145464.pdf

The Idea School. (2018). Why The Idea School. Retrieved from https://www.theideaschool.org/why-the-idea-school

The National Research Council. (2018). Three-dimensional learning. *Next Generation Science Standards*. Retrieved from http://www.nextgenscience.org/glossary

Tsupros, N., Kohler, R., & Hallinen, J. (2009). STEM education: A project to identify the missing components. *Intermediate Unit 1: Center for STEM Education and Leonard Gelfand Center for Service Learning and Outreach*. Pittsburgh, PA: Carnegie Mellon University.

Wardrip, P. S. & Brahms, L. (2016). Taking making to school. In K. Peppler, E.R. Halverson, & Y.B. Kafai. (Eds.). *Makeology: Makerspaces as Learning Environments, 1*, p. 97-106.

INDEX

YOUR OPINION MATTERS:
TELL US HOW WE'RE DOING!

Your feedback helps ISTE create the best possible resources for teaching and learning in the digital age. Share your thoughts with the community or tell us how we're doing!

YOU CAN:

➤ Write a review at amazon.com or barnesandnoble.com.

➤ Mention this book on social media and follow ISTE on Twitter @iste, Facebook @ISTEconnects or Instagram @isteconnects.

➤ Email us at books@iste.org with your questions or comments.